Marco Colombo

LPIC-1 102-500 Practice Exams

**250 Questions and Answers to test
your knowledge**

2020

First Printing: 2020

ISBN: 978-0-244-26589-2

Contents

Acknowledgment

And here I am again writing thanks. Let's say this is the sweetest moment when I can express my feelings. Writing a book is very tiring, but thanks to the support of fantastic people like my parents and my girlfriend, the effort seems to be halved.

A heartfelt thanks also to the Linux Professional Institute who believed in me and gave me the opportunity to became an LPI Publishing Partner and to collaborate with them in the preparation of some LPI Learning Materials for Linux Essentials and LPIC-1 certifications.

Finally, a dutiful thanks goes to all my readers, followers, and supporters who bought the first book. You have been many, much more than I could have hoped for. Waking up in the morning and seeing that someone had purchased a copy of the book made me proud. Someone had believed in me. The private messages received asking me if there would be a second part in the future, the Facebook group that grew day by day, and the thanks of those who had passed the first exam were a stimulus to write and publish this new book. And now, I sincerely hope not to disappoint those who were waiting for it and that these exam simulations can be of help to all future penguins who decide to obtain the LPIC-1 certification.

Impressum

This publication meets the requirements of the Linux Professional Institute Publishing Partner (LPP) program. Authors, editors and publishers hereby undertake that the present publication covers the stated learning objectives of the exam(s) covered of the version current at the time of publication. These learning objectives are presented in a complete, technically sound manner and in a form suitable for exam preparation. Visit https://learning.lpi.org to learn more about the LPP program and provide feedback on this publication.

Preface

The Linux Professional Institute has developed a multi-level Linux professional certification program for people who deal with the Linux world. The LPIC-1 certification is the first certification in this program and, to become LPIC-1 certified, you must pass both the LPI 101 and LPI 102 exams. At the time of publication, the version is 5.0 and the exam codes are 101-500 and 102-500.

Through this book you have the opportunity to practice and test your knowledge before taking the LPI 102 exam. You can find the objectives of the exam, defined by the Linux Professional Institute, and a collection of 250 questions and answers, divided into four practice exams and one assessment test.

Each practice exam simulates a real LPI 102 exam and its questions, as well as those of the assessment test, have been designed as useful exercises to focus on the main topics and improve Linux skills and abilities. In addition, a detailed explanation of each question allows you to see not only the correct answer, but also the general context to which the question refers.

Please rememeber that the questions you find in this book are not the original questions of a real LPI 102 exam. Also remember that the questions are not brain dumps and that the author of the book does not endorse any kind of brain dump.

Exam 102-500 Objectives

Topic 105: Shells and Shell Scripting

105.1 Customize and use the shell environment (Weight 4)

Description:

Candidates should be able to customize shell environments to meet users' needs. Candidates should be able to modify global and user profiles.

Key Knowledge Areas:

- Set environment variables (e.g. PATH) at login or when spawning a new shell.

- Write Bash functions for frequently used sequences of commands.

- Maintain skeleton directories for new user accounts.

- Set command search path with the proper directory.

Partial list of the used files, terms and utilities:

., source, /etc/bash.bashrc, /etc/profile, env, export, set, unset, ~/.bash_profile, ~/.bash_login, ~/.profile, ~/.bashrc, ~/.bash_logout, function, alias

105.2 Customize or write simple scripts (Weight 4)

Description:

Candidates should be able to customize existing scripts, or write simple new Bash scripts.

Key Knowledge Areas:

- Use standard sh syntax (loops, tests).

- Use command substitution.

- Test return values for success or failure or other information provided by a command.

- Execute chained commands.

- Perform conditional mailing to the superuser.

- Correctly select the script interpreter through the shebang (#!) line.

- Manage the location, ownership, execution and suid-rights of scripts.

Partial list of the used files, terms and utilities:

for, while, test, if, read, seq, exec, ||, &&

Topic 106: User Interfaces and Desktops

106.1 Install and configure X11 (Weight 2)

Description:

Candidates should be able to install and configure X11.

Key Knowledge Areas:

- Understanding of the X11 architecture.

- Basic understanding and knowledge of the X Window configuration file.

- Overwrite specific aspects of Xorg configuration, such as keyboard layout.

- Understand the components of desktop environments, such as display managers and window managers.

- Manage access to the X server and display applications on remote X servers.

- Awareness of Wayland.

Partial list of the used files, terms and utilities:

/etc/X11/xorg.conf, /etc/X11/xorg.conf.d/, ~/.xsession-errors, xhost, xauth, DISPLAY, X

106.2 Graphical Desktops (Weight 1)

Description:

Candidates should be aware of major Linux desktops. Furthermore, candidates should be aware of protocols used to access remote desktop sessions.

Key Knowledge Areas:

- Awareness of major desktop environments.
- Awareness of protocols to access remote desktop sessions.

Partial list of the used files, terms and utilities:

KDE, Gnome, Xfce, X11, XDMCP, VNC, Spice, RDP

106.3 Accessibility (Weight 1)

Description:

Demonstrate knowledge and awareness of accessibility technologies.

Key Knowledge Areas:

- Basic knowledge of visual settings and themes.
- Basic knowledge of assistive technology.

Partial list of the used files, terms and utilities:

High Contrast/Large Print Desktop Themes, Screen Reader, Braille Display, Screen Magnifier, On-Screen Keyboard, Sticky/Repeat keys, Slow/Bounce/Toggle keys, Mouse keys, Gestures, Voice recognition

Topic 107: Administrative Tasks

107.1 Manage user and group accounts and related system files (Weight 5)

Description:

Candidates should be able to add, remove, suspend and change user accounts.

Key Knowledge Areas:

- Add, modify and remove users and groups.

- Manage user/group info in password/group databases.

- Create and manage special purpose and limited accounts.

Partial list of the used files, terms and utilities:

/etc/passwd, /etc/shadow, /etc/group, /etc/skel/, chage, getent, groupadd, groupdel, groupmod, passwd, useradd, userdel, usermod

107.2 Automate system administration tasks by scheduling jobs (Weight 4)

Description:

Candidates should be able to use cron and systemd timers to run jobs at regular intervals and to use at to run jobs at a specific time.

Key Knowledge Areas:

- Manage cron and at jobs.

- Configure user access to cron and at services.

- Understand systemd timer units.

Partial list of the used files, terms and utilities:

/etc/cron.{d,daily,hourly,monthly,weekly}/, /etc/at.deny, /etc/at.allow, /etc/crontab, /etc/cron.allow, /etc/cron.deny, /var/spool/cron/,crontab, at, atq, atrm, systemctl, systemd-run

107.3 Localisation and internationalisation (Weight 3)

Description:

Candidates should be able to localize a system in a different language than English. As well, an understanding of why LANG=C is useful when scripting.

Key Knowledge Areas:

- Configure locale settings and environment variables.

- Configure timezone settings and environment variables.

Partial list of the used files, terms and utilities:

/etc/timezone, /etc/localtime, /usr/share/zoneinfo/, LC_*, LC_ALL, LANG, TZ, /usr/bin/locale, tzselect, timedatectl, date, iconv, UTF-8, ISO-8859, ASCII, Unicode

Topic 108: Essential System Services

108.1 Maintain system time (Weight 3)

Description:

Candidates should be able to properly maintain the system time and synchronize the clock via NTP.

Key Knowledge Areas:

- Set the system date and time.

- Set the hardware clock to the correct time in UTC.

- Configure the correct timezone.

- Basic NTP configuration using ntpd and chrony.

- Knowledge of using the pool.ntp.org service.

- Awareness of the ntpq command.

Partial list of the used files, terms and utilities:

/usr/share/zoneinfo/,   /etc/timezone,   /etc/localtime,   /etc/ntp.conf,
/etc/chrony.conf, date, hwclock, timedatectl, ntpd, ntpdate, chronyc, pool.ntp.org

108.2 System logging (Weight 4)

Description:

Candidates should be able to configure rsyslog. This objective also includes configuring the logging daemon to send log output to a central log server or accept log output as a central log server. Use of the systemd journal subsystem is covered. Also, awareness of syslog and syslog-ng as alternative logging systems is included.

Key Knowledge Areas:

- Basic configuration of rsyslog.

- Understanding of standard facilities, priorities and actions.

- Query the systemd journal.

- Filter systemd journal data by criteria such as date, service or priority.

- Configure persistent systemd journal storage and journal size.

- Delete old systemd journal data.

- Retrieve systemd journal data from a rescue system or file system copy.

- Understand interaction of rsyslog with systemd-journald.

- Configuration of logrotate.

- Awareness of syslog and syslog-ng.

Partial list of the used files, terms and utilities:

/etc/rsyslog.conf,   /var/log/,   logger,   logrotate,   /etc/logrotate.conf,
/etc/logrotate.d/,   journalctl,   systemd-cat,   /etc/systemd/journald.conf,
/var/log/journal/

108.3 Mail Transfer Agent (MTA) basics (Weight 3)

Description:

Candidates should be aware of the commonly available MTA programs and be able to perform basic forward and alias configuration on a client host. Other configuration files are not covered.

Key Knowledge Areas:

- Create e-mail aliases.

- Configure e-mail forwarding.

- Knowledge of commonly available MTA programs (postfix, sendmail, exim) (no configuration).

Partial list of the used files, terms and utilities:

~/.forward, sendmail emulation layer commands, newaliases, mail, mailq, postfix, sendmail, exim

108.4 Manage printers and printing (Weight 2)

Description:

Candidates should be able to manage print queues and user print jobs using CUPS and the LPD compatibility interface.

Key Knowledge Areas:

- Basic CUPS configuration (for local and remote printers).

- Manage user print queues.

- Troubleshoot general printing problems.

- Add and remove jobs from configured printer queues.

Partial list of the used files, terms and utilities:

CUPS configuration files, tools and utilities, /etc/cups/, lpd legacy interface (lpr, lprm, lpq)

Topic 109: Networking Fundamentals

109.1 Fundamentals of internet protocols (Weight 4)

Description:

Candidates should demonstrate a proper understanding of TCP/IP network fundamentals.

Key Knowledge Areas:

- Demonstrate an understanding of network masks and CIDR notation.
- Knowledge of the differences between private and public "dotted quad" IP addresses.
- Knowledge about common TCP and UDP ports and services (20, 21, 22, 23, 25, 53, 80, 110, 123, 139, 143, 161, 162, 389, 443, 465, 514, 636, 993, 995).
- Knowledge about the differences and major features of UDP, TCP and ICMP.
- Knowledge of the major differences between IPv4 and IPv6.
- Knowledge of the basic features of IPv6.

Partial list of the used files, terms and utilities:

/etc/services, IPv4, IPv6, Subnetting, TCP, UDP, ICMP

109.2 Persistent network configuration (Weight 4)

Description:

Candidates should be able to manage the persistent network configuration of a Linux host.

Key Knowledge Areas:

- Understand basic TCP/IP host configuration.
- Configure ethernet and wi-fi network using NetworkManager.
- Awareness of systemd-networkd.

Partial list of the used files, terms and utilities:

/etc/hostname, /etc/hosts, /etc/nsswitch.conf, /etc/resolv.conf, nmcli, hostnamectl, ifup, ifdown

109.3 Basic network troubleshooting (Weight 4)

Description:

Candidates should be able to troubleshoot networking issues on client hosts.

Key Knowledge Areas:

- Manually configure network interfaces, including viewing and changing the configuration of network interfaces using iproute2.

- Manually configure routing, including viewing and changing routing tables and setting the default route using iproute2.

- Debug problems associated with the network configuration.

- Awareness of legacy net-tools commands.

Partial list of the used files, terms and utilities:

ip, hostname, ss, ping, ping6, traceroute, traceroute6, tracepath, tracepath6, netcat, ifconfig, netstat, route

109.4 Configure client side DNS (Weight 2)

Description:

Candidates should be able to configure DNS on a client host.

Key Knowledge Areas:

- Query remote DNS servers.

- Configure local name resolution and use remote DNS servers.

- Modify the order in which name resolution is done.

- Debug errors related to name resolution.

- Awareness of systemd-resolved.

Partial list of the used files, terms and utilities:

/etc/hosts, /etc/resolv.conf, /etc/nsswitch.conf, host, dig, getent

Topic 110: Security

110.1 Perform security administration tasks (Weight 3)

Description:

Candidates should know how to review system configuration to ensure host security in accordance with local security policies.

Key Knowledge Areas:

- Audit a system to find files with the suid/sgid bit set.
- Set or change user passwords and password aging information.
- Being able to use nmap and netstat to discover open ports on a system.
- Set up limits on user logins, processes and memory usage.
- Determine which users have logged in to the system or are currently logged in.
- Basic sudo configuration and usage.

Partial list of the used files, terms and utilities:

find, passwd, fuser, lsof, nmap, chage, netstat, sudo, /etc/sudoers, su, usermod, ulimit, who, w, last

110.2 Setup host security (Weight 3)

Description:

Candidates should know how to set up a basic level of host security.

Key Knowledge Areas:

- Awareness of shadow passwords and how they work.

- Turn off network services not in use.

- Understand the role of TCP wrappers.

Partial list of the used files, terms and utilities:

/etc/nologin, /etc/passwd, /etc/shadow, /etc/xinetd.d/, /etc/xinetd.conf, systemd.socket, /etc/inittab, /etc/init.d/, /etc/hosts.allow, /etc/hosts.deny

110.3 Securing data with encryption (Weight 4)

Description:

The candidate should be able to use public key techniques to secure data and communication.

Key Knowledge Areas:

- Perform basic OpenSSH 2 client configuration and usage.

- Understand the role of OpenSSH 2 server host keys.

- Perform basic GnuPG configuration, usage and revocation.

- Use GPG to encrypt, decrypt, sign and verify files.

- Understand SSH port tunnels (including X11 tunnels).

Partial list of the used files, terms and utilities:

gpg, gpg-agent, ~/.gnupg/, ssh, ssh-keygen, ssh-agent, ssh-add, ~/.ssh/authorized_keys, ssh_known_hosts, ~/.ssh/id_rsa and id_rsa.pub, /etc/ssh/ssh_host_rsa_key and ssh_host_rsa_key.pub, ~/.ssh/id_dsa and id_dsa.pub, /etc/ssh/ssh_host_dsa_key and ssh_host_dsa_key.pub, ~/.ssh/id_ecdsa and id_ecdsa.pub, /etc/ssh/ssh_host_ecdsa_key and ssh_host_ecdsa_key.pub, ~/.ssh/id_ed25519 and id_ed25519.pub, /etc/ssh/ssh_host_ed25519_key and ssh_host_ed25519_key.pub.

Assessment Test

1. You want to list all timer units including inactive ones. Which of the following commands can you use to accomplish this task? Assume that your Linux system uses systemd as system and service manager.

    A. timerd list --all

    B. timerctl show-timers --all

    C. lstimer --all

    D. systemctl list-timers --all

2. What's the meaning of the following line in **/etc/sudoers**?

    ```
    kevin ALL=(ALL) NOPASSWD: ALL
    ```

    A. The user named **kevin** can log into the system without typing his password

    B. The user named **kevin** can run a command that requires root privileges with **sudo** without typing his password

    C. All the users in the system, except **kevin**, can run a command that requires root privileges with **sudo** without typing their personal password

    D. All the users in the system, except **kevin**, can run a command that requires root privileges with **sudo** without typing the root password

3. Which of the following fields cannot be found in the **/etc/group** file?

   A. The group name

   B. A comma-delimited list of usernames of the group members, except those for whom this is the primary group

   C. A comma-delimited list of UIDs (User IDs) of the group members, except those for whom this is the primary group

   D. The Group ID (GID)

4. Using **nmcli**, you want to disable Wi-Fi. Which of the following commands can you use?

   A. nmcli radio wifi off

   B. nmcli wifi disable

   C. nmcli connection wifi disable

   D. nmcli status wifi off

5. Acting as root, you are editing the **/etc/chrony.conf** configuration file on a machine that is often not connected to the Internet at startup. Which of the following options of the **server** directive can you use to indicate that the time source server should not be contacted until **chronyd** receives notification that the link to the Internet is present?

   A. wait

   B. offline

   C. iburst

   D. delay_polling

6. Your Linux machine has several displays to allow users to perform graphic works simultaneously. Which of the following statements is true?

    A. Every X server has a display name in the form of **hostname:username.displaynumber**

    B. Every X server has a display name in the form of **hostname:displaynumber.username**

    C. Every X server has a display name in the form of **hostname:username.screennumber**

    D. Every X server has a display name in the form of **hostname:displaynumber.screennumber**

7. In the current bash shell you defined the aliases for your most used commands, but you do not remember them all. Which of the following commands can you use to review them?

    A. lsaliases

    B. lsalias

    C. alias

    D. aliases

8. You are editing **/etc/rsyslog.conf**. Which of the following lines can you use to send all kernel log messages to **/var/log/kern.log**?

    A. kern.* /var/log/kern.log

    B. *.kern /var/log/kern.log

    C. kern,* /var/log/kern.log

    D. *,kern /var/log/kern.log

9. You want to connect to the OpenSSH server with IP address 192.168.1.10 using the **admin** user when accessing the remote server. Which of the following commands can you use? Assume that the OpenSSH server is listening for connection requests on port 2112.

   A. ssh --user admin --port 2112 192.168.1.10

   B. ssh -u admin -p 2112 192.168.1.10

   C. ssh -p 2112 admin@192.168.1.10

   D. ssh -o ConnectionPort=2112 admin@192.168.1.10

10. Working with the bash shell, you want to test if the **foobar** file exists and is a regular file. Which of the following commands can you use?

   A. test -d foobar && echo "I's a regular file" || echo "Not a regular file"

   B. test -r foobar && echo "I's a regular file" || echo "Not a regular file"

   C. test -f foobar && echo "I's a regular file" || echo "Not a regular file"

   D. test -e foobar && echo "I's a regular file" || echo "Not a regular file"

Answers to the Assessment Test

1. D - Topic 107.2

The **systemctl** command is used to control the systemd system and service manager. In particular, the **list-timers** subcommand lists the active timer units, ordered by the time they elapse next. To see all timers, including inactive ones, you can use the **-a** or **--all** option, making option D the correct answer. For completeness, the **timerd**, **timerctl** and **lstimer** commands do not exist.

2. B - Topic 110.1

The **/etc/sudoers** file determines the users' **sudo** privileges on a Linux system. In this file you can find user specifications and aliases (for example, groups of users and groups of commands), which determine which tasks different users can perform using the **sudo** command (who may run what). The line in the question refers to the **kevin** user account and basically specifies that this user can run any command (the last **ALL**) on any host (the first **ALL**) as any user (the **ALL** within round brackets) without typing his password (**NOPASSWD**). Therefore, **kevin** can run a command that requires root privileges with **sudo** without being asked to insert his password. This makes option B the correct answer.

3. C - Topic 107.1

In Linux, **/etc/group** is a file of four colon-delimited fields that contains basic information about groups. Each line describes a single group and contains the following fields: **Group Name**, **Group Password** (the encrypted password of the group, or an **x** if shadow passwords are used), **Group ID** (GID - the numeric group ID), and **a comma-delimited list of usernames of the group members,**

except those for whom this is the primary group. Therefore, option C is the correct answer.

4. A - Topic 109.2

In Linux, **nmcli** is a command-line tool for controlling NetworkManager and reporting network status. In particular, you can use the **nmcli radio wifi** command to show the Wi-Fi status, the **nmcli radio wifi on** command to enable Wi-Fi, and the **nmcli radio wifi off** command to disable Wi-Fi (in general the **radio** object is used to show radio switches status, or to enable and disable the switches). Therefore, option A is the correct answer. For completeness, the **nmcli** command does not have the **wifi** and **status** objects, and the **connection** object does not have the **wifi** subcommand (in general the **connection** object is used to start, stop, and manage network connections).

5. B - Topic 108.1

In **/etc/chrony.conf**, the **server** directive specifies an NTP server (by name or IP address), which can be used as a time source. This directive supports a lot of options like **iburst** that is used to allow **chronyd** to make the first update of the clock shortly after startup, and **offline** that is used to tell **chronyd** not to poll the server until it is enabled to do so (thus when the link to the Internet is present and the server is reachable). Therefore, option B is the correct answer. For completeness, the **wait** and **delay_polling** options do not exist.

6. D - Topic 106.1

From the user's perspective, every X server has a display name in the form of: **hostname:displaynumber.screennumber**, where **hostname** is the name of the client machine to which the display is physically connected (if not specified, the most efficient way of communicating to a server on the same machine is used), **displaynumber** is the number of the display on the client machine starting at 0 which is assigned when the X server for that display is started (the term **display** usually refers to a collection of monitors that share a common keyboard and pointer), and **screennumber** is the number of the screen starting at 0 which is used to identify a single monitor when the X server for that display is started (if not specified, **screen 0** is used). Therefore, option D is the correct answer.

7. C - Topic 105.1

An alias is usually used to define new command names that are easy to remember, create command shortcuts that avoid typing long commands, and implement some command options as a default. To review all the aliases defined in the current bash shell, you can use the **alias** command, making option C the correct answer.

8. A - Topic 108.2

In Linux, **/etc/rsyslog.conf** is the main configuration file for **rsyslog**. The syntax for each line in this file is as follows: **facility.priority action**, where **facility** is the subsystem that generates a specific log message (* means all facilities), **priority** is the importance of the message (* means all priorities), and **action** is the file (or other location) in which to save log messages (* means the terminals of all connected users). Therefore, option A is the correct answer.

9. C - Topic 110.3

In Linux, to connect to a remote machine, you can use the **ssh remote-machine** command, where **remote-machine** can be an IP address or a machine name. This command uses the current user when accessing the remote server and therefore if you want to specify a different username for the SSH connection, you need to use the following syntax: **ssh user@remote-machine**. Finally, you can specify a different port number with the **-p** (or **-o Port=**) option. As a result, the right command to use is **ssh -p 2112 admin@192.168.1.10** (or alternatively **ssh -o Port=2112 admin@192.168.1.10**). This makes option C the correct answer.

10. C - Topic 105.2

The **test** command is a bash built-in that is used to evaluate conditional expressions. It exits with a status of 0 if the result of the test is true or 1 if the result is false. In particular, the **-f** unary operator is used to perform a simple test on a specific filesystem object and returns true if this object exists and is a regular file, making option C the correct answer. For completeness, the **-e** unary operator returns true if the specified filesystem object exists, the **-d** unary operator returns true if the specified filesystem object exists and is a directory, and the **-r** unary operator returns true if the specified filesystem object exists and is readable. Finally, remember that you can build a minimal but complete conditional test by using the **&&** operator for the **true branch** and the **||** operator for the **false branch**.

102-500
Practice Exams

Practice Exam 1

1. Working with bash, you want to write a script named **foo.sh** which prints the first and third variables passed to the script on the screen. Which of the following commands can you use inside your bash script (after the **shebang line**)? Assume that **foo.sh** has the execution bit set correctly.

    A. echo $0 $2

    B. echo $0,2

    C. echo $1,3

    D. echo $1 $3

2. Using X.org-X11, you want to add the machine with static IP address 192.168.1.10 to the list of machines from which your X server accepts connections. Which of the following commands can you use?

    A. xhost --allow=192.168.1.10

    B. xhost +

    C. xhost 192.168.1.10

    D. xadd +192.168.1.10

    E. xadd --allow=192.168.1.10

3. What is the broadcast address for the 192.168.4.0/22 network?

4. You mistakenly created a new user account in the system and now you need to change its username from **foo.bar** to **bar.foo**. Which of the following commands can you use? Assume you are acting as root.

    A. usermod -l bar.foo foo.bar

    B. usermod -l foo.bar bar.foo

    C. usermod --login-name foo.bar bar.foo

    D. usermod --login-name bar.foo foo.bar

5. By checking the **/etc/shadow** file, you notice that the **foobar** user account was accidentally locked. Which of the following commands can you use to unlock it? Assume that your system uses shadow passwords. Select two.

    A. chage -U foobar

    B. passwd -u foobar

    C. chage -u foobar

    D. usermod -U foobar

    E. unlock foobar

6. You are working in a 192.168.1.0/24 network and you want to configure a host by assigning it the IP address 192.168.1.150 and the netmask 255.255.255.0 on the fly. Which of the following commands can you use? Assume you are acting as root.

    A. ip link set 192.168.1.150/24

    B. ip addr add 192.168.1.150/24 dev eth0

    C. ip link address 192.168.1.150 255.255.255.0 dev eth0

    D. ip addr set 192.168.1.150 255.255.255.0

7. Acting as root, you are configuring the **xinetd** super daemon so that your system has a global configuration file for general settings and uses the files in **/etc/xinetd.d** as specific configuration files for each service managed by **xinetd**. Which of the following lines can you insert in the configuration file of a specific service managed by **xinetd** to temporary disable it?

   A. enable = no

   B. active = no

   C. disable = yes

   D. inactive = yes

8. Working with bash, you define two shell variables named **FOO** and **BAR** and then you launch the **hello.sh** script that you have previously created (see the extract below).

```
$ FOO=Hello
$ BAR=World
$ cat hello.sh
#!/bin/bash
echo $FOO $BAR
$ ./hello.sh
```

What is the result? Assume that the script has the execution bit set correctly.

   A. Hello World

   B. $FOO $BAR

   C. FOO BAR

   D. An error

   E. An empty line

9. Working with bash, you want to remove the shell variables named **foo**, **bar**, **foobar** and **barfoo** that you have mistakenly created. Which of the following commands can you use?

   A. remove foo, bar, foobar, barfoo

   B. unset foo bar foobar barfoo

   C. remove foo bar foobar barfoo

   D. unset foo, bar, foobar, barfoo

   E. You cannot remove multiple variables using a single command

10. The ordinary user named **foo** wants to run the **foobar.sh** script every day at 01:00 am. Which of the following **crontab** entries can he use?

    A. 0 1 * * 0 /home/foo/foobar.sh

    B. 1 0 * * * /home/foo/foobar.sh

    C. 0 1 * * * /home/foo/foobar.sh

    D. 1 0 * * 0 /home/foo/foobar.sh

11. The **foo** user wants to create a script named **foobar.sh** making sure that the output is not passed through **locale translations**. How can he accomplish this task?

    A. He defines **LANG=C** at the beginning of the script

    B. He defines **LOCALE=DEFAULT** at the beginning of the script

    C. He defines **TRANSLATE=no** at the beginning of the script

    D. He defines **LOCALE=no** at the beginning of the script

    E. He defines **LC=ALL** at the beginning of the script

12. You want to restrict access to **at** and **batch** commands for some users. Which of the following files can you use to accomplish this task?

    A. **/etc/at.allow** and **/etc/at.deny**

    B. **/etc/at/user.allow** and **/etc/at/user.deny**

    C. **/etc/allow/at.user** and **/etc/deny/at.user**

    D. **/etc/at/allow-user** and **/etc/at/deny-user**

    E. **/etc/user-allow** and **/etc/user-deny**

13. Working with the bash shell, the **root** user types the **su foobar** command in his home directory (**/root** with permissions **rwx------**) and then, as **foobar**, types **ls -l**. What is the result? Assume that the original login session is that of **root**.

    A. All files and directories in the **/home/foobar** directory are displayed

    B. All files and directories in the **/root** directory are displayed

    C. All files and directories in the **/** directory are displayed

    D. A permission denied error is displayed

14. In Linux, **/etc/shadow** is a file of nine colon-delimited fields that contains the encrypted passwords of the users, each on a separate line. Which of the following fields can you find in this file? Select two.

    A. The user username

    B. The Group ID (GID) of the user

    C. The User Id (UID) of the user

    D. Last password change

    E. A comma-delimited list of users belonging to the primary group of the user

15. You are working in a small network with few Linux machines and you have not configured a DNS server for local name resolution. Which of the following files that provides static mapping of IP addresses to hostnames should you always keep up to date on individual computers? Assume you are acting as root.

    A. /etc/hostname

    B. /etc/resolv.conf

    C. /etc/hosts

    D. /etc/host-mapping

16. You are working in a 192.168.100.224/29 network. How many IP addresses can you use for configuring your hosts?

    A. The network provided is not valid

    B. 8

    C. 14

    D. 6

    E. 10

17. Using systemd, you want to search through the journal log files. Which of the following utilities can you use? Assume you are acting as root.

    A. journal-search

    B. log-search

    C. logctl

    D. journalctl

    E. logjournal

18. How can you express the 255.255.255.200 netmask using the CIDR notation?

    A. /25

    B. /26

    C. /27

    D. The netmask provided is not valid

19. You want to know the routing path to the network host with IP address 192.168.1.155. Which of the following commands can you use?

    A. ping

    B. hostpath

    C. host

    D. traceroute

20. Given the following line in **/etc/nsswitch.conf**:

```
hosts:      files dns
```

What can you deduce?

    A. The **/etc/hosts** file is consulted first for name resolution

    B. The **/etc/hostname** file is consulted first for name resolution

    C. The configured DNS servers are consulted first for name resolution

    D. The **/etc/nsswitch.conf** is misconfigured; the **hosts** line does not exist (the right line is **order**)

21. You want to convert the **foobar** file from the ISO8859-2 code set to the UTF-8 code set by redirecting the output to a new file named **barfoo**. What command can you use? Write only the command name without options or arguments.

22. On modern Linux systems, **/etc/localtime** is simply a symbolic link to a specific time zone file. Which of the following directories contains the files that store information for all available time zones?

    A. /usr/timezone/zoneinfo

    B. /usr/timezone

    C. /usr/share/zoneinfo

    D. /usr/share/timezone

23. You try to ping the host **www.yourdomain.com**, but it seems not to respond. What could be the most probable network issue?

    A. The network card of the host is broken

    B. The network card of your machine is broken

    C. You have a DNS problem; your DNS servers are probably unreachable

    D. The host **www.yourdomain.com** does not exist (there is probably a typo)

24. Which of the following statements about GPG keys is true?

    A. GPG keys are generated using the **gpg-keygen** command and are stored in a keyring in the **~/.gnupg** directory

    B. GPG keys are generated using the **gpg --gen-key** command and are stored in a keyring in the **~/.gnupg** directory

    C. GPG keys are generated using the **gpg-keygen** command and are stored in a keyring in the **~/.gpg/keyring** directory

    D. GPG keys are generated using the **gpg --gen-key** command and are stored in a keyring in the **~/.gpg/keyring** directory

25. To secure your system, you want to find all the regular files with the SUID or SGID bits set. Which of the following commands can you use? Assume that you are using an old Linux distribution (thus with an old version of **findutils**) and that you are acting as root.

    A. find / -perm +6000 -type f

    B. find / -perm +4000 -type f

    C. find / -suid -sgid -type f

    D. find / -auth ug -type f

    E. find / -auth suid,sgid -type f

26. You are working in a 192.200.100.224/29 network. Which of the following IP addresses can be assigned to hosts within your network? Select two.

    A. 192.200.100.231

    B. 192.200.100.230

    C. 192.200.100.225

    D. 192.200.100.224

    E. 192.200.100.248

27. You want to test basic connectivity between two hosts using the **ping** command. Which of the following options can you use if you want to send only five packets to the specified destination host? Assume that no deadline is set.

    A. -C

    B. -N

    C. -c

    D. -n

28. The **foo** user wants to examine all the errors logged by the X Window system that occur within his Linux graphical environment. Which of the following files can he check?

    A. ~/.xsession-errors

    B. /etc/X11/Xsession/Xerrors

    C. ~/.Xerrors

    D. /etc/X11/Xerrors/Xsession/err.log

29. You want to take the network interface eth0 down. Which of the following commands can you use?

    A. iface eth0 disable

    B. ifdisable eth0

    C. ifdown eth0

    D. iface down eth0

30. Working with the bash shell, you type **seq -s: 5 3 10**. What will be the output of this command?

    A. 5:8

    B. 5:8:10

    C. 8:5

    D. 10:8:5

31. In the bash shell, you have defined the aliases for your most used commands. Among these, an alias has been defined for the **rm** command (**alias rm="rm -i"**), which prevents the accidental deletion of important files. What command can you use to remove this alias? Write the complete command.

32. What is stored in the fourth and sixth fields of **/etc/passwd**?

    A. The User ID (fourth field) and Group ID (sixth field) of each user

    B. The Group ID (fourth field) and home directory (sixth field) of each user

    C. The username (fourth field) and password (sixth field) of each user

    D. The home directory (fourth field) and shell (sixth field) of each user

33. Acting as root, you type **date 02030830** on the command line. What will be the result?

    A. The software clock will be set at 08:30 am on February 3rd of the current year

    B. The software clock will be set at 08:30 am on March 2nd of the current year

    C. The software clock will be set at 02:03 am on August 30th of the current year

    D. The software clock will be set at 03:02 am on August 30th of the current year

    E. You will get a syntax error

34. Using **nmcli**, you want to display all your connections. Which of the following commands can you use?

    A. nmcli show connections -a

    B. nmcli list con

    C. nmcli con show

    D. nmcli list connections -a

35. You are writing a bash script that takes a number between 1 and 5 as input and performs a particular action based on this value. Which of the following constructs can you use in your shell script to implement this list of possibilities?

    A. for

    B. case

    C. while

    D. seq

36. Which of the following is not a MTA? Select two.

    A. exerc

    B. sendmail

    C. exim

    D. postmail

    E. postfix

37. Acting as root, you want to set the system time from the hardware clock so that both the system clock and the hardware clock are synchronized. Which of the following commands can you use? Select two.

    A. hwclock --setsys

    B. hwclock --systohc

    C. hwclock --hctosys

    D. hwclock -w

    E. hwclock -s

    F. hwclock -z

38. You want to prevent system logins by ordinary users. What can you do to achieve this goal? Assume you are acting as root.

    A. Remove the **/etc/login** file

    B. Put the **NOLOGIN 1** line in the **/etc/login/security.conf** file

    C. Put the **LOGIN FALSE** line in the **/etc/security/confparameters** file

    D. Create the **/etc/nologin** file

39. In Linux, **nmcli** is a command-line tool that operates on a series of objects. Which of the following is valid? Select two.

    A. link

    B. connector

    C. radio

    D. host

    E. device

40. The **foo** user created a **.forward** file in his home directory with only the **|~/bar** line inside it. What does this line mean?

    A. Nothing. It is not a valid configuration

    B. All the incoming e-mails of **foo** are forwarded to the **bar** user on the same machine

    C. All the incoming e-mails of **foo** are piped to the **~/bar** program

    D. The incoming e-mails of **foo** marked as spam are forwarded to the **bar** user on the same machine

    E. The incoming e-mails of **foo** marked as spam are piped to the **~/bar** program

41. When bash is invoked as an interactive login shell, it first reads and executes commands from the **/etc/profile** file, if that file exists (along with any **.sh** files in **/etc/profile.d**). What happens next?

   A. It looks for the **~/.bashrc** and **~/.bash.bashrc** files, in that order, and reads and executes commands from the first one that exists and is readable

   B. It looks for the **~/.bashrc_profile**, **~/.bashrc_login** and **~/.profile** files, in that order, and reads and executes commands from the first one that exists and is readable

   C. It looks for the **~/.bash_profile**, **~/.bash_login**, and **~/.profile** files, in that order, and reads and executes commands from the first one that exists and is readable

   D. It looks for the **~/.bash_login** and **~/.bashrc** files, in that order, and reads and executes commands from the first one that exists and is readable

42. You have the following two lines in your **/etc/ntp.conf** file:

```
server  ntp.domain.com
server  ntp.domain1.com
```

   What can you deduce?

   A. The server **ntp.domain.com** will be used as the primary time source

   B. The server **ntp.domain1.com** will be used as the primary time source

   C. The server **ntp.domain1.com** will be used as the primary time source only if **ntp.domain.com** is down

   D. There is no way to know which server will be used as the primary time source; your local computer will use the server that provides the cleanest time data

43. The **foo** user wants to schedule a new **crontab job**. What is the best way to do this? Assume that **foo** is working with the bash shell.

    A. He opens his own **crontab file** with his favorite text editor (for example **vi**) and then edits it directly

    B. He uses the **cronedit** command with the **-e** option

    C. He uses the **crontabs** command with the **-e** option

    D. He uses the **crontab** command with the **-e** option

44. You want to call the **foobar** command with standard output and standard error connected to the journal. Which of the following commands can help you accomplish this task? Assume that your Linux system uses systemd as system and service manager.

    A. systemd-log

    B. systemd-cat

    C. journalctl-log

    D. logger-cat

45. Which of the following statements about **Sticky Keys** accessibility feature is true?

    A. It can be useful for users who tend to press a single key accidentally multiple times

    B. It enables users to use the keyboard's numeric keypad as a pointing device to emulate the mouse

    C. It can be useful for users who accidentally press several keys at a time while typing

    D. It can be useful for users who have difficulty holding down two or more keys simultaneously

46. Which of the following is a network login protocol that can handle remote logins? Assume you are using X Window System for remote access.

    A. XDPCP

    B. XDMCP

    C. XSSHCP

    D. XFCP

47. Acting as root, you want to set that members of the **sys-admin** group can execute all programs with root privileges using the **sudo** command without typing their password. Which of the following configuration files should you edit?

    A. /etc/visudo.conf

    B. /etc/sudoers

    C. /etc/sudo/sudoers.conf

    D. /etc/sudo/visudo

48. Which of the following facilities can you use in the **rsyslog** main configuration file? Select three.

    A. notice

    B. kern

    C. local0

    D. local10

    E. local7

49. Acting as root, you want to change the listening port of your OpenSSH server. Which configuration file should you edit? Write the full path.

50. You are editing **/etc/rsyslog.conf**. Which of the following lines can you use to send all mail log messages with priority **info** or higher to **/var/log/mail.log**?

    A. mail.=info /var/log/mail.log

    B. mail.info /var/log/mail.log

    C. info mail /var/log/mail.log

    D. info =mail /var/log/mail.log

51. You want to print the **foobar.txt** file to the printer named **Print_office_1**. Which of the following options of the **lpr** command can you use to specify this particular printer? Assume that **Print_office_1** is not the default printer on your BSD-compatible system.

    A. -p

    B. -P

    C. --printer-name

    D. -r

52. You are using **CUPS** printing system. What is the name of its main configuration file and which file contains all the printer definitions and configurations?

    A. **cups.conf** (the main configuration file) and **lpr.conf** (the file containing all the printer definitions and configurations)

    B. **cupsd.conf** (the main configuration file) and **printers.conf** (the file containing all the printer definitions and configurations)

    C. **cupsd.conf** (the main configuration file) and **lpr.conf** (the file containing all the printer definitions and configurations)

    D. **cups.conf** (the main configuration file) and **printers.conf** (the file containing all the printer definitions and configurations)

53. Acting as root, you want to know the groups to which the **foo** user belongs. Which of the following commands can you use? Select two.

    A. group foo

    B. groups foo

    C. id foo

    D. lsuser foo

    E. user foo

54. You want to perform a DNS lookup. Which of the following utilities can help you accomplish this task?

    A. dnslookup

    B. host

    C. searchdns

    D. queryd

55. Acting as root, you want to add a new mail alias for the **foobar** user. What should you do after adding this new alias to the mail alias database file? Assume you are using postfix as a mail server.

    A. Run the **newaliases** command

    B. Run the **reload-alias** command and restart the mail server

    C. Run the **updatealias** command

    D. Run the **alias-reload** command

    E. Nothing; the change takes effect immediately

56. You have defined the **foobar.timer** file, which controls the **foobar.service** unit. Which of the following lines can you find inside **foobar.timer** if **foobar.service** runs every day at 06.00 am?

   A. OnCalendar=* * * * 06:00:00 *

   B. OnCalendar=*-*-* 06:00:00

   C. OnCalendar=00 06 * * *

   D. OnCalendar=00 06 * * * *

57. Which of the following statements about **/etc/hosts.allow** and **/etc/hosts.deny** is true?

   A. These files are used by **initx** to look for machines that are authorized or not to access a specific service

   B. These files are used by **xinetd** to look for machines that are authorized or not to access a specific service

   C. These files are used by **TCP Wrappers** to look for machines that are authorized or not to access a specific service

   D. These files are used by **xconn** to look for machines that are authorized or not to access a specific service

58. Alice wants to send an encrypted file to Bob. Which of the following statements is true? Assume that both Alice and Bob use GPG.

   A. Alice must have Bob's GPG private key before encrypting the file

   B. Alice must have Bob's GPG public key before encrypting the file

   C. Alice and Bob must exchange their GPG private keys

   D. Bob must have Alice's GPG private key to decrypt the file

59. The **foo** user wants to create a new authentication key pair for SSH (a new private and public key) to be used to connect to a remote OpenSSH server without providing any password (**foo** will not enter the passphrase during the generation of the keys). Which of the following commands can he use?

    A. genkey-ssh

    B. ssh-genkey

    C. ssh-keygen

    D. sshkey

60. The **last** command is used to list recent logins and logouts on a Linux system. Where does the data displayed by this command come from?

    A. The data is pulled from the **/var/log/ltmp** file

    B. The data is pulled from the **/var/log/dtmp** file

    C. The data is pulled from the **/var/log/wtmp** file

    D. The data is pulled from the **/var/log/utmp** file

Practice Exam 2

1. Working with bash, you define two shell variables named **FOO** and **BAR** and then you launch the **hello.sh** script that you have previously created (see the extract below).

```
$ export FOO=Hello
$ export BAR=World
$ cat hello.sh
#!/bin/bash
echo $FOO $BAR
$ ./hello.sh
```

   What is the result? Assume that the script has the execution bit set correctly.

   A. Hello World

   B. $FOO $BAR

   C. An empty line

   D. An error

2. You have changed the listening port of your OpenSSH server. Which system-wide configuration file should you edit as root on OpenSSH client machines to connect to this new port? Assume that you maintain a global configuration file for each OpenSSH client machine, and that no user on those machines has their own ssh configuration file in their home directory. Write the full path of the file.

3. You are editing **/etc/rsyslog.conf**. Which of the following lines can you use to send all mail log messages with only priority **info** to **/var/log/mail.log**?

    A. mail.=info /var/log/mail.log

    B. mail.info /var/log/mail.log

    C. info =mail /var/log/mail.log

    D. =info mail /var/log/mail.log

4. Which of the following addresses is reserved for private networks? Select two.

    A. 192.186.100.10

    B. 192.168.250.15

    C. 172.168.10.10

    D. 172.16.5.30

    E. 130.172.5.55

5. Which of the following statements about an interactive bash shell (that is not a login shell) is true?

    A. When it is started, bash reads and executes commands from the **~/.bash_login** script, if that file exists

    B. When it is started, bash reads and executes commands from the **~/.bash_profile** script, if that file exists

    C. When it is started, bash reads and executes commands from the **~/.bashrc** script, if that file exists

    D. When it is started, bash reads and executes commands from the **~/.bashrc_login** script, if that file exists

6. You want to get information about the current **locale environment**. Which of the following commands can you use?

   A. setlocale

   B. locale

   C. envlocale

   D. showlocale

7. Given the following routing table:

   ```
   default via 192.168.5.1 dev eth0
   192.168.5.0/24 dev eth0 proto kernel scope link src 192.168.5.10
   ```

   Which of the following statements is true?

   A. An outgoing packet to the destination host 192.168.5.100 is transmitted to the default gateway 192.168.5.1

   B. An outgoing packet to the destination host 192.168.5.100 is transmitted directly to the host over eth0

   C. An outgoing packet to the destination host 192.168.5.100 is transmitted to the default gateway 192.168.5.0

   D. An outgoing packet to the destination host 192.168.5.100 is rejected because the default route is not set

8. You want to restrict access to **cron** for some users. Which of the following files can you use to accomplish this task? Assume you are acting as root.

   A. **/etc/crontab.allow** and **/etc/crontab.deny**

   B. **/etc/crontab/user.allow** and **/etc/crontab/user.deny**

   C. **/etc/cron.allow** and **/etc/cron.deny**

   D. **/etc/cron/user.allow** and **/etc/cron/user.deny**

9. You want to show the contents of your mail queue. Which of the following commands can you use in a **sendmail compatible MTA**?

    A. mailq

    B. lsmail

    C. lsqueue

    D. sendmail -bi

10. Acting as root, you want to set the hardware clock to the current system time so that both the system clock and the hardware clock are synchronized. Which of the following commands can you use? Select two.

    A. hwclock --systohc

    B. hwclock -t

    C. hwclock --hctosys

    D. hwclock -w

    E. hwclock -s

    F. hwclock --syshc

11. Working as a system administrator, you create a user named **foo_usr** using the **useradd -m foo_usr** command. By default, which of the following directories holds the files that are copied into the home directory of **foo_usr** when this account is created? Assume that you have not set a custom directory in **/etc/default/useradd**.

    A. /etc/login

    B. /etc/bashrc/skeleton_dir

    C. /etc/skel

    D. /etc/profile/skel

12. Working with bash, you want to assign the result of the arithmetic expression **10 + 5** to the shell variable named **VAR**. Which of the following commands can you use?

    A. let VAR=10+5

    B. let $VAR=10+5

    C. VAR=10+5

    D. VAR=10+5;export VAR

13. The **LANG** environment variable normally holds the current language (indicated as the **locale**) of a Linux system. Which of the following is a valid value for this variable?

    A. English

    B. UTF-8_EN

    C. it_IT.UTF-8

    D. Europe/Paris

14. Acting as root, you are editing the **/etc/chrony.conf** configuration file. Which of the following options of the **server** directive can you use to allow **chronyd** to make the first update of the clock shortly after startup?

    A. speed

    B. iburst

    C. quick-sync

    D. fastsync

    E. driftstart

15. Given the following **crontab** entry:

```
10 11 * * 0,1 foobar
```

What does it mean?

    A. **foobar** runs at 10:11 am on Monday and Tuesday

    B. **foobar** runs at 10:11 am on Sunday and Monday

    C. **foobar** runs at 11:10 am on Sunday and Monday

    D. **foobar** runs at 11:10 am on Monday and Tuesday

16. Acting as root, you are configuring a specific service managed by the **xinetd** super daemon. Which of the following attributes can you use in this **xinetd** configuration file to bind the service to a specific interface on your Linux machine? Select two.

    A. only_from

    B. bind

    C. interface

    D. iface

    E. inet_addr

17. You want to filter the journal logs, showing only entries with **warning** or higher priority. Which of the following commands can you use?

    A. journalctl --since=warning --until=emerg

    B. journalctl --from=warning --to=emerg

    C. journalctl --range warning-emerg

    D. journalctl -p warning

    E. journalctl -r warning

18. Which of the following command-line tools is a front end for NetworkManager that can be used by both users and scripts?

    A. nmtui

    B. nmcli

    C. nmctl

    D. nmcmd

19. What is the effect of the following command?

```
chage -M 30 days
```

    A. It sets that all users must change their password every 30 days

    B. It sets that all users must change their password at least once every 30 days

    C. It sets to 30 the maximum number of days that must pass before a password change is required for the user account named **days**

    D. It sets that the user account named **days** will be disabled after 30 days of inactivity

20. Acting as root, you create an ordinary user named **foo** with the **useradd** command and assign him the bash login shell. However, **foo** prefers tcsh to bash and wants to change his default login shell. What can this ordinary user do? Assume that the tcsh shell is listed in **/etc/shells**.

    A. He cannot change his login shell. He can only ask you or other users with root privileges to do it

    B. He can use the **chsh -s /bin/tcsh** command

    C. He can edit the **/etc/passwd** file directly

    D. He can use the **usermod -s /bin/tcsh foo** command

21. You want to modify all **locale categories** at once without changing the system language (the **LANG** environment variable). Which of the following variables do you need to edit and export?

   A. LOCALE_ALL

   B. LOCALE_*

   C. LC_*

   D. LC_ALL

22. Which of the following sequences represents the correct increasing order for priorities to keep in mind when editing the **/etc/rsyslog.conf** file?

   A. debug - notice - info - warning - err - crit - alarm - emerg

   B. debug - info - notice - warning - err - emerg - alert - crit

   C. debug - info - notice - warning - err - crit - alarm - emerg

   D. debug - notice - info - warning - alarm - err - crit - emerg

   E. debug - info - notice - warning - err - crit - alert - emerg

23. In your system, each server that should be run via **xinetd** uses a specific file with its own configuration options. Which of the following directories contains all these files?

   A. /etc/xinetd/xtcpd.d

   B. /etc/xtcpd/xinetd.d

   C. /etc/xinetd.d

   D. /etc/xinetd/sockets.d

24. The **bar** user wants mail sent to him to be temporarily forwarded to an external address. Which of the following files can this ordinary user edit to accomplish this task?

    A. /home/bar/aliases

    B. /home/bar/.forward

    C. /etc/aliases

    D. He can't do this. He must ask the system administrator for help

25. You want to add a new connection using the **nmcli** command. Which of the following connection types (**connection.type** property or **type** alias) is valid? Select two.

    A. eth0

    B. wlan0

    C. wifi

    D. bridge

    E. dialup

26. Working with bash, you want to make the shell variable named **var_foobar** visible (thus usable) in child processes generated by the current shell. Which of the following commands can you use? Select two.

    A. define -x var_foobar

    B. export var_foobar

    C. export $var_foobar

    D. declare -x var_foobar

    E. create $var_foobar

27. You want to show the current print queue status on the printer named **Print_office_1**. Which of the following commands can you use? Assume you are using a BSD-compatible system.

    A. lprq

    B. lpq

    C. lsqueue

    D. lq

28. You want to list only the listening UDP ports on your Linux system. Which of the following options of the **netstat** command can help you accomplish this task?

    A. -au

    B. -lt

    C. -st

    D. -lu

29. Given the following **OnCalendar** entry in **foo.timer**:

```
*:0/1
```

What does it mean? Assume that you have already created the matching **foo.service** file.

    A. The service runs every hour

    B. The service runs every second

    C. The service runs every minute

    D. It is not a valid specification

30. You want to start a stopped printer, deleting all its queued jobs. Which of the following options of the **cupsenable** command can you use? Assume that your machine uses CUPS printing system.

    A. -c

    B. -d

    C. -C

    D. -D

31. Which of the following files contains the public keys that can be used to log in as the **foo** user account on a remote OpenSSH server using public key authentication?

    A. The **/home/foo/.sshd/public.keys** file on the remote OpenSSH server

    B. The **/home/foo/.sshd/keys.allow** file on the remote OpenSSH server

    C. The **/home/foo/.ssh/authorized_keys** file on the remote OpenSSH server

    D. The **/home/foo/.ssh/managed_keys** file on the remote OpenSSH server

32. Working with bash, you want to print the Process ID of the current shell and the exit code of the last command. Which of the following commands can you use to accomplish this task?

    A. echo "Process ID Current Shell: $! - Exit Code Last Command: $EXIT"

    B. echo "Process ID Current Shell: $$ - Exit Code Last Command: $?"

    C. echo "Process ID Current Shell: $PID - Exit Code Last Command: $!"

    D. echo "Process ID Current Shell: $PPID - Exit Code Last Command: $$"

    E. echo "Process ID Current Shell: $PID - Exit Code Last Command: $EXIT"

33. Acting as root, you want to configure the local name resolution for the **foo** host with IP address 192.168.5.10. Which of the following lines should you put in the **/etc/hosts** file to accomplish this task? Assume that you are working in a small network and that no DNS servers have been configured.

    A. 192.168.5.5   foo.domain.org   foo

    B. foo   foo.domain.org   192.168.5.5

    C. foo.domain.org   192.168.5.5   foo

    D. foo.domain.org   foo   192.168.5.5

34. Working with the bash shell, what is the output of the following command?

```
echo 'This sequence is put in 4 variables' | while read var1 var2 var3 var4; do
echo $var4 $var3 $var2 $var1; done
```

    A. This sequence is put in 4 variables

    B. variables 4 in put is sequence This

    C. put in 4 variables is sequence This

    D. put in 4 variables This sequence is

    E. put is sequence This

35. Acting as root, you want to add the user named **bar** to the group **foobar**. Which of the following commands can you use?

    A. add2group -a foobar bar

    B. gpasswd -a bar foobar

    C. gpasswd -a foobar bar

    D. add2group -a bar foobar

36. Which of the following statements about the **hostname** command is true?

    A. It can be used by users with root privileges to permanently set the hostname of the local machine

    B. It can be used by users with root privileges to temporarily set the hostname of the local machine

    C. It can be used by all users to permanently set the hostname of the local machine

    D. It can be used by all users to temporarily set the hostname of the local machine

37. You want to set up an NTP server. Which public NTP server pool can you use as a time source for your server?

    A. public.server-ntp.org

    B. pool.server-ntp.org

    C. public.ntp.org

    D. pool.ntp.org

38. Which of the following statements about the **netstat** legacy net tool is true? Select three.

    A. It can be used to display interface statistics

    B. It can be used to print network connections

    C. It can be used to add and delete routes

    D. It can be used to display the kernel routing tables

    E. It can be used to configure a network interface

39. You want to connect to the OpenSSH server with IP address 192.168.1.10 using your user account when accessing the remote server. Which of the following commands can you use? Assume that the OpenSSH server is listening for connection requests on port 2112.

    A. ssh 192.168.1.10:2112

    B. ssh 192.168.1.10/2112

    C. ssh -p tcp/2112 192.168.1.10

    D. ssh -o Port=2112 192.168.1.10

40. Using X.org-X11, you want to edit the **xorg.conf** file to save and test a new configuration. Which of the following lines, located at the beginning of one of the major sections, can you find in this file? Select two.

    A. Section "Monitor"

    B. Section "ServiceLayout"

    C. Section "InputDevice"

    D. Section "Keyboard_Pointer"

    E. Section "Modules"

41. Which of the following is a Display Manager? Select two.

    A. XDM

    B. LightDM

    C. XgreeterDM

    D. KromeDM

    E. XPLOREDM

42. You want to run a graphical application on a Linux machine with IP address 192.168.5.10, but a very small monitor is connected to it. So you decide to redirect its output to another Linux machine with IP address 192.168.1.100 because it has a more adequate monitor to work with. Which of the following commands should you type on the bash shell of the Linux machine with IP address 192.168.5.10 before running the graphical application? Assume that you sit on the machine with IP address 192.168.1.100 and you connect via SSH to the bash shell of the machine with IP address 192.168.5.10. Also assume that the machine with IP address 192.168.5.10 has been added to the list of machines from which the X server on the machine with IP address 192.168.1.100 accepts connections.

    A. export $DISPLAY 192.168.5.10:0

    B. export DISPLAY 192.168.5.10:0

    C. export DISPLAY 192.168.1.100:0

    D. export $DISPLAY 192.168.1.100:0

43. Which of the following statements about an IPv6 address is true?

    A. An IPv6 address is 128-bit long

    B. An IPv6 address is 64-bit long

    C. An IPv6 address is 32-bit long

    D. An IPv6 address is 16-bit long

44. Given the following lines:

```
search foo.com
nameserver 192.168.1.10
nameserver 192.168.0.10
```

Which configuration file are you looking at? Write the full path.

45. Acting as root, while trying to unmount a filesystem, you get an error message telling you that the device is busy. Which of the following commands can help you find out which processes are accessing the filesystem, thus preventing its proper unmount? Select two.

    A. lsop

    B. fuser

    C. listproc

    D. lsof

    E. fpo

46. The **foo** user has forgotten his password and so asks the system administrator to change it. Which of the following commands can the administrator use?

    A. chpass foo

    B. chpass -u foo

    C. passwd foo

    D. passwd -u foo

47. Acting as root, you want to configure some system-wide mail aliases. Which of the following files should you edit to accomplish this task?

    A. /etc/alias.conf

    B. /etc/mail/alias.conf

    C. /etc/aliases/mail.conf

    D. /etc/aliases

48. Acting as root, you want to change the order in which your Linux system performs name resolution. What file should you edit? Write only the file name.

49. Which of the following statements about known TCP ports 21 and 22 is true?

    A. The HTTP service is assigned to TCP port 21, while the HTTPS service is assigned to TCP port 22

    B. The SMTP service is assigned to TCP port 21, while the IMAP service is assigned to TCP port 22

    C. The FTP service is assigned to TCP port 21, while the SSH service is assigned to TCP port 22

    D. The Telnet service is assigned to TCP port 21, while the POP3 service is assigned to TCP port 22

50. You want to delete the **at job** identified by job number 10 that you have previously scheduled. Which of the following commands can you use to accomplish this task? Select two.

    A. atrm 10

    B. atdel 10

    C. at --remove 10

    D. at -r 10

    E. at --delete 10

51. What are the equivalent commands for **ping** and **traceroute** for IPv6 addresses?

    A. **pingv6** and **traceroutev6**

    B. **ping-6** and **traceroute-6**

    C. **ping6** and **traceroute6**

    D. **pingip6** and **tracerouteip6**

52. When writing a script, you usually need to add the so-called **shebang** line to identify the shell used to run the script. Which of the following characters does the **shebang** line start with?

    A. #!

    B. !#

    C. #$

    D. $#

53. You are writing a script named **foobar.sh** that performs some useful tasks and, for each of them, you want to log the start time, end time, and some comments for debugging purposes. Which of the following commands can help you make entries in the system log? Assume that your Linux machine uses the traditional **syslog** system log module.

    A. logger

    B. printlog

    C. logr

    D. envlog

54. You want to set some resource usage limits of your bash shell, including the maximum size of files you can create with it. Which of the following commands can you use to accomplish this task?

    A. ulimit

    B. slimit

    C. rlimits

    D. climits

55. Which of the following accessibility technologies can help blind or visually impaired users working on Linux distributions?

    A. Screen Recorders

    B. Screen Readers

    C. Translation Tools

    D. Bluetooth and Wireless keyboards

56. You are using a Linux system with shadow passwords. Which of the following statements is true?

    A. You have better security because ordinary users cannot read password hashes

    B. You have better security because both the **/etc/passwd** and **/etc/shadow** files cannot be read by ordinary users

    C. You have better security because both the **/etc/group** and **/etc/gshadow** files cannot be read by ordinary users

    D. You have better security because ordinary users cannot use a password equal to one of the previous five

    E. You have better security because the system does not accept passwords with less than eight characters

57. Which of the following is a plain ASCII file that provides a mapping between internet network services and their assigned port numbers and protocol types?

    A. /etc/mapping

    B. /etc/services

    C. /etc/portmapping

    D. /etc/ports

58. You want to sign the **foo.txt** file, leaving the contents in plaintext (thus still readable). Which of the following options of the **gpg** command can you use?

    A. --sign

    B. --clearsign

    C. --plaintext

    D. --psign

    E. --cleartext

59. You want to set the host 192.168.10.1 as the default gateway for your machine. Which of the following commands can you use to make this configuration on the fly? Assume you are acting as root.

    A. ip route add default via 192.168.10.1 dev eth0

    B. ip route add default gw 192.168.10.1 dev eth0

    C. ip link set 192.168.10.1 default via dev eth0

    D. ip link set 192.168.10.1 default gw dev eth0

60. Which of the following statements about the **useradd** command is true?

    A. If used with the **-h** option, it creates a new user account with a custom home directory

    B. If used with the **-k** option, it creates a new user account with a specific login shell

    C. If used with the **-g** option, it creates a new user account by adding it to the specified secondary groups

    D. If used with the **-u** option, it creates a new user account with a specific User ID (UID)

Practice Exam 3

1. Given the following:

```
#!/bin/bash
VAR=0;
if [ $# -lt 1 ]; then VAR=1; else VAR=2; fi
echo $VAR;
```

What's the meaning of this simple script?

   A. It prints **1** if you call the script with one or without parameters; otherwise it prints **2**

   B. It prints **1** if you call the script with one or more parameters; otherwise it prints **2**

   C. It prints **1** if you call the script with one parameter; otherwise it prints **2**

   D. It prints **1** if you call the script without parameters; otherwise it prints **2**

2. Acting as root, you want to create a new group named **web_developers**. Which of the following commands can you use to accomplish this task?

   A. newgroup web_developers

   B. newgrp web_developers

   C. groupmod --add web_developers

   D. groupadd web_developers

3. Working with bash, you want to put the output of the **pwd** command into the shell variable named **current_path**. Which of the following commands can you use?

    A. current_path='${pwd}'

    B. current_path='$(pwd)'

    C. current_path="${pwd}"

    D. current_path="$(pwd)"

4. Which of the following curses-based TUI applications is a front end for NetworkManager?

    A. nmcli

    B. nmtui

    C. nmconfig

    D. tuiconfig

    E. cliconfig

5. You want to add the **/usr/games** and **/opt/custom** directories to the **PATH** variable permanently so that you don't need to specify a fully qualified path each time you execute an application in these directories. Working with bash, which of the following lines do you need to put inside your shell startup files?

    A. export PATH=PATH:/usr/games:/opt/custom

    B. export $PATH=$PATH:/usr/games:/opt/custom

    C. export $PATH=PATH:/usr/games:/opt/custom

    D. export PATH=$PATH:/usr/games:/opt/custom

6. You are writing a bash script named **TestDir.sh** that tests if the first parameter passed to the script is a directory and if so, it prints "**It's a directory**", otherwise it prints "**Not a directory**". Which of the following commands can you use in your bash script? Don't worry about the preliminary checks of the script (it ends if you enter two or more parameters or no parameters).

    A. test -f $1 && echo "It's a directory" || echo "Not a directory"

    B. test -L $1 && echo "It's a directory" || echo "Not a directory"

    C. test -d $1 && echo "It's a directory" || echo "Not a directory"

    D. test -e $1 && echo "It's a directory" || echo "Not a directory"

7. Acting as root, you want to set up the DNS servers used for name resolution. Which of the following files should you edit?

    A. /etc/dnsconfig

    B. /etc/resolv.conf

    C. /etc/dnsresolver

    D. /etc/resolver.conf

8. Acting as root on your Debian system, you decide to remove the user account named **foo** because he no longer uses this machine. Which of the following commands can you use? Assume that you also want to remove the home directory and the mail spool of this user account.

    A. userdel -r foo

    B. rm -r foo

    C. rmuser -r foo

    D. delusr -r foo

9. You want to change your system time zone once you arrive in Madrid. Which of the following is the valid time zone specification you can set?

    A. Europe/Spain/Madrid

    B. Europe/Madrid

    C. EU/SP/Madrid

    D. Spain/Madrid

10. Given the following routing table:

Destination	Gateway	Genmask	Flags	Metric	Ref	Use	Iface
0.0.0.0	192.168.1.254	0.0.0.0	UG	0	0	0	eth0
192.168.1.0	0.0.0.0	255.255.255.0	U	0	0	0	eth0
192.168.5.0	0.0.0.0	255.255.255.0	U	0	0	0	eth1
192.168.10.0	192.168.1.100	255.255.255.0	UG	0	0	0	eth0

What can you deduce?

    A. An outgoing packet to the destination host 192.168.10.100 is transmitted to the router 192.168.1.100, which isn't the default gateway of the system

    B. An outgoing packet to the destination host 192.168.10.100 is transmitted to the default gateway 192.168.1.100

    C. An outgoing packet to the destination host 192.168.10.100 is transmitted to the router 192.168.1.254, which isn't the default gateway of the system

    D. An outgoing packet to the destination host 192.168.10.100 is transmitted to the default gateway 192.168.1.254

    E. An outgoing packet to the destination host 192.168.10.100 is transmitted directly to the host over eth0

    F. An outgoing packet to the destination host 192.168.10.100 is transmitted directly to the host over eth1

11. In Linux **/etc/passwd** is a file that stores the account information of each user in the system. Which of the following entries can you find in this file? Assume that your system uses shadow passwords.

    A. foobar:x:1000:foobar: foobar linux user:/home/foobar:/bin/bash

    B. foobar:x:1000:1000: foobar linux user:/bin/bash:/home/foobar

    C. foobar:x:1000: foobar linux user:/home/foobar:/bin/bash

    D. foobar:x:1000:1000:foobar linux user:/home/foobar:/bin/bash

12. Given the following **crontab** entry:

```
*/15 * * * * foobar
```

What does it mean?

    A. **foobar** runs every fifteen days

    B. **foobar** runs every fifteen minutes

    C. **foobar** runs every fifteen hours

    D. **foobar** runs every fifteen months

13. You want to print five copies of the **foobar.txt** file. Which of the following options of the **lpr** command can help you set the number of copies to print? Assume you are using a BSD-compatible system.

    A. -$

    B. -k

    C. -#

    D. -m

    E. -!

14. Acting as root, you are looking at the contents of **/etc/aliases**. Which of the following entries is valid for this file? Select two.

    A. root fooadmin

    B. bar: foobar, barfoo

    C. bar: foobar$barfoo

    D. bar foobar barfoo

    E. foo: /home/foo/mail-folder

15. Which of the following addresses is reserved for private networks? Select two.

    A. 10.10.10.10

    B. 172.31.22.22

    C. 127.127.10.5

    D. 132.168.100.50

    E. 192.68.55.55

16. The IP address of your host is 192.168.7.100 with netmask 255.255.255.0. What is the network address?

17. When trying to resolve **www.yourdomain.com**, the DNS servers specified in **/etc/resolv.conf** provide an IP address that seems incorrect. How can you verify the result? Assume you are using the **dig** utility.

    A. dig -s 8.8.8.8 www.yourdomain.com

    B. dig @8.8.8.8 www.yourdomain.com

    C. dig --debug www.yourdomain.com

    D. dig -o query-all www.yourdomain.com

18. Given the following bash extract:

```
# foo=bar
# echo $foo
bar
# alias foovalue="echo The value of foo is $foo"
# foo=foobar
```

What is the result if you type **foovalue** in the bash shell? Assume you are acting as root.

    A. The value of foo is foobar

    B. The value of foo is bar

    C. The value of foo is $foo

    D. An error: the **alias** command cannot be used with shell variables

19. Working with the bash shell, you type **su - foobar**. What will be displayed on the bash prompt after entering the correct password for **foobar**? Assume that the **PS1** environment variable for **foobar** is only set in the following files: **/home/foobar/.bashrc**, **/home/foobar/.profile**, **/home/foobar/.bash_login**, and **/home/foobar/.bash_profile**.

    A. The bash prompt will display information according to the value of the **PS1** environment variable set in the **/home/foobar/.bash_profile** file

    B. The bash prompt will display information according to the value of the **PS1** environment variable set in the **/home/foobar/.bash_login** file

    C. The bash prompt will display information according to the value of the **PS1** environment variable set in the **/home/foobar/.profile** file

    D. The bash prompt will display information according to the value of the **PS1** environment variable set in the **/home/foobar/.bashrc** file

20. You want to run a graphical application on a Linux machine with IP address 192.168.5.10, but a very small monitor is connected to it. So you decide to redirect its output to another Linux machine with IP address 192.168.1.100 because it has a more adequate monitor to work with. You sit on the machine with IP address 192.168.1.100 and you connect via SSH to the bash shell of the machine with IP address 192.168.5.10, but when you launch the graphical application, you receive the message "Can't open Display". How can you resolve? Assume that you have correctly exported the **DISPLAY** variable.

   A. You have to run the **xhost 192.168.5.10** command on the computer with IP address 192.168.1.100

   B. You have to run the **xhost 192.168.1.100** command on the computer with IP address 192.168.5.10

   C. You have to run the **xhost 192.168.5.10** command on the computer with IP address 192.168.5.10

   D. You have to run the **xhost 192.168.1.100** command on the computer with IP address 192.168.1.100

21. Which of the following statements about the **netcat** utility is true? Select two.

   A. It uses only the TCP protocol

   B. It uses only the UDP protocol

   C. It uses both TCP and UDP protocols

   D. It can be used to send data across network connections

   E. It cannot be used with scripts

22. In which user or group management file could you find this entry? Write the full path.

   jacob:!:18071:0:99999:7:::

23. Which of the following programs that holds private keys for public key authentication and their passphrase can be useful for a user who wants to automatically log in to a remote OpenSSH server multiple times during a local session typing the passphrase only once and not every time? Assume that the server has the public key of the user and that a passphrase has been entered during the generation of the keys to increase the security.

    A. ssh-log

    B. ssh-session

    C. ssh-auth

    D. ssh-agent

24. Acting as root, you want to impose a limit on how many times the **foo** user can log into the system. Which of the following configuration files should you edit? Assume that your login sever is using PAM.

    A. /etc/pam/limits.conf

    B. /etc/pam/ulimit

    C. /etc/security/limits.conf

    D. /etc/security/ulimit

25. Working with bash, you want to assign the value of the **VAR1** variable to the **VAR2** variable. Which of the following commands can you use?

    A. VAR2=VAR1

    B. VAR2=$VAR1

    C. VAR2=$(VAR1)

    D. VAR1 > VAR2

26. You want to display the list of all available **locales** on your system. Which of the following options of the **locale** command can you use?

    A. --list-locales

    B. -l

    C. --all-locales

    D. -s

27. What is the IPv6 address for localhost?

    A. ::ff80

    B. ::fe00

    C. ::1

    D. 127.0.0.1

28. Which of the following statements about Xorg-X11 is true?

    A. The main configuration file is **Xorg-X11.conf** and is divided into several sections, each of which begins with the keyword **Section** and ends with **EndSection**

    B. The main configuration file is **xorg.conf** and is divided into several sections, each of which begins with the keyword **Section** and ends with **EndSection**

    C. The main configuration file is **Xorg-X11.conf** and is divided into several sections, each of which has a specific name and consists of a series of lines enclosed within curly braces

    D. The main configuration file is **xorg.conf** and is divided into several sections, each of which has a specific name and consists of a series of lines enclosed within curly braces

29. You want to show who is currently logged into the system. Which of the following commands can you use to accomplish this task? Select two.

    A. who

    B. w

    C. wis

    D. wc

    E. wislogged

30. You want to trace the path to a network host, discovering MTU along this path. Which of the following commands can you use?

    A. mpath

    B. mtutrace

    C. ptrace

    D. tracepath

31. Acting as root, you are configuring the **xinetd** super daemon so that your system has a global configuration file for general settings and uses the files in **/etc/xinetd.d** as specific configuration files for each service managed by **xinetd**. What is the name of this global configuration file?

    A. /etc/xinetd.conf

    B. /etc/security/xinetd.conf

    C. /etc/xinetd/service.conf

    D. /etc/xinetd/security.conf

    E. /etc/security.conf

32. Which of the following statements about the Telnet service is true?

    A. It is assigned to UDP port 23

    B. It is assigned to TCP port 23

    C. It is assigned to UDP port 123

    D. It is assigned to TCP port 123

33. Which of the following statements about the **ip** command is true? Select two.

    A. It can be used to add a new route on the fly

    B. It can be used to set the hostname of the system on the fly

    C. It can be used to perform DNS lookups

    D. It can be used to permanently change the order in which name resolution is performed

    E. It can be used to assign an IP address to a network interface on the fly

34. You want to set up a route for the 10.10.10.0/24 network for which packets destined to this network should be passed through the 192.168.1.1 router, which isn't the default gateway for your system. Which of the following commands can you use?

    A. ip route add 10.10.10.0/24 via 192.168.1.1 dev eth0

    B. ip route add -net 10.10.10.0/24 -gw 192.168.1.1 dev eth0

    C. ip route add -net 10.10.10.0/24 -via 192.168.1.1 dev eth0

    D. route add -net 10.10.10.0 -netmask 255.255.255.0 -gw 192.168.1.1 -dev eth0

    E. route add -net 10.10.10.0 -netmask 255.255.255.0 -via 192.168.1.1 -dev eth0

35. You want to create a custom script named **foobar.sh** that uses a different time zone than the one set on your machine. What can you do?

    A. Define the **TZ** environment variable

    B. Define the **LANG** environment variable

    C. Edit **/etc/localtime** manually by entering the time zone you want to use (such as **Europe/Rome**) and then launch the script

    D. You can't do this. A script always uses the time zone of your machine

36. The **barfoo** user wants to forward his mail to the external addresses **bar@mydomain.com** and **foo@mydomain.com**, but also keep a copy in his local mailbox. Which of the following lines should **barfoo** put into the **.forward** file in his home directory?

    A. $barfoo & bar@mydomain.com & foo@mydomain.com

    B. \barfoo, bar@mydomain.com, foo@mydomain.com

    C. $barfoo, bar@mydomain.com, foo@mydomain.com

    D. $barfoo && bar@mydomain.com && foo@mydomain.com

    E. barfoo & bar@mydomain.com & foo@mydomain.com

    F. \barfoo && bar@mydomain.com && foo@mydomain.com

37. The **foo** user has difficulty using a regular keyboard, but can use a mouse. Which of the following accessibility technologies can help him?

    A. A screen reader

    B. The Mouse Keys accessibility feature

    C. The on-screen keyboard

    D. A screen magnifier application

38. Which of the following statements about the **sendmail** command is true?

    A. It is deprecated and has been replaced by the **postq** command

    B. If launched with the **-bp** option, it allows you to reconfigure the MTA installed on your system

    C. It is provided for compatibility reasons by many MTAs

    D. If launched with the **-bp** option, it allows you to reconfigure the MTA installed on your system only if it is **sendmail,** otherwise you get an error

39. Working with the bash shell, you want to declare a read-only variable named **max_count** and assign it a value of 999. Which of the following commands can you use?

    A. declare --read-only max_count=999

    B. declare -r max_count;max_count=999

    C. declare -r max_count=999

    D. declare -R max_count=999

40. You want to show log messages from a specific boot on your machine. Which of the following options of the **journalctl** command can you use to accomplish this task? Assume you are acting as root.

    A. -b

    B. -n

    C. --boot-select

    D. --boot-number

41. You are editing the **/etc/resolv.conf** configuration file. What keyword can you use in this file to add a new server for name resolution? Write only the keyword name.

42. The **foo** user receives a signed **foobar.gpg** file and wants to verify its signature. Which of the following commands can he use to accomplish this task? Assume that **foo** has the correct key in his keyring to verify the signature.

    A. gpg --check foobar.gpg

    B. gpg --check-signature foobar.gpg

    C. gpg --verify foobar.gpg

    D. gpg --verify-signature foobar.gpg

43. Acting as root, you are configuring a specific service managed by the **xinetd** super daemon. Which of the following attributes can you use in this **xinetd** configuration file to specify the remote hosts to which the service is available?

    A. access_from

    B. allow

    C. restrict

    D. only_from

44. Which of the following are typical pairs of private and public user keys? Assume that OpenSSH clients and servers are configured to use only protocol 2.

    A. **~/.ssh/id_dsa.pri** and **~/.ssh/id_dsa.pub**

    B. **~/.ssh/id_ed25519** and **~/.ssh/id_ed25519.pub**

    C. **/etc/ssh/ssh_host_rsa_key.pri** and **/etc/ssh/ssh_host_rsa_key.pub**

    D. **/etc/ssh/ssh_host_ecdsa_key** and **/etc/ssh/ssh_host_ecdsa_key.pub**

45. You want to configure persistent systemd journal storage. What option do you need to modify in your **journald.conf** configuration file? Assume you are acting as root. Write only the option name.

46. You are using a Linux system with shadow passwords. Which of the following statements is true?

    A. The **x** character is stored in the second field of **/etc/passwd** and **/etc/group** instead of encrypted user and group passwords

    B. The **$** character is stored in the second field of **/etc/passwd** and **/etc/group** instead of encrypted user and group passwords

    C. The **?** character is stored in the second field of **/etc/passwd** and **/etc/group** instead of encrypted user and group passwords

    D. The **%** character is stored in the second field of **/etc/passwd** and **/etc/group** instead of encrypted user and group passwords

47. Acting as root, you want to find out who has scheduled **at jobs** in the system. Which of the following commands can you use?

    A. at -l

    B. at -r

    C. at -f

    D. at -v

48. You want to back up your GPG public keyring. Which of the following files do you need to copy and archive to accomplish this task? Assume that you are using the legacy version of GnuPG (version 1.4).

    A. ~/.gnupg/secring.gpg

    B. ~/.gnupg/sec.keyring

    C. ~/.gnupg/pubring.gpg

    D. ~/.gnupg/pub.keyring

49. Using an old Linux distribution, you want to perform a manual time synchronization by setting the system time to the time maintained by an NTP server. Which of the following commands can you use? Assume you are acting as root.

    A. sysclock

    B. ntpdate

    C. ntpclock

    D. ntp-sync

50. Acting as root, you want to add a new entry to **/etc/crontab**. Which of the following syntaxes should you use?

    A. Minute Hour Month Day_of_month Day_of_week Account Command

    B. Minute Hour Day_of_month Month Day_of_week Account Command

    C. Minute Hour Day_of_week Day_of_month Month Year Command

    D. Minute Hour Day_of_month Month Day_of_week Year Command

    E. Hour Minute Month Day_of_month Day_of_week Account Command

    F. Hour Minute Month Day_of_month Day_of_week Year Command

51. Which of the following combinations of **facility** and **priority** can you use to indicate all log messages generated by a system? Assume that you are editing **/etc/rsyslog.conf**.

    A. ALL.ALL

    B. *:*

    C. ALL:ALL

    D. *.*

52. Using **nmcli**, you want to list the available Wi-Fi access points (known to NetworkManager) to connect to. Which of the following commands can you use to accomplish this task?

    A. nmcli wifi show

    B. nmcli interface wifi list

    C. nmcli device wifi list

    D. nmcli con wifi show

    E. nmcli wifi list

53. Which of the following is a Linux Desktop Environment? Select two.

    A. GDM

    B. GNOME

    C. KDM

    D. Xfce

    E. Exim

54. The **netstat** command can be used as a useful auditing tool within a network. Which of the following options of this command can you use to show both listening and non-listening sockets?

    A. --all

    B. --all-sockets

    C. --display-all

    D. --all-connections

55. Which of the following directives should you use in **/etc/ntp.conf** or **/etc/chrony.conf** to specify an NTP server that can act as a time source?

    A. ntp-server

    B. source-server

    C. server

    D. source

    E. time-source

56. Which of the following permissions are typically set on **/etc/passwd** and **/etc/shadow**? Assume that your system uses shadow passwords and that the owner and group for these files is **root**.

    A. rw-rw-rw- on **/etc/passwd** and r--r--r-- on **/etc/shadow**

    B. rw------- on **/etc/passwd** and rw-r--r-- on **/etc/shadow**

    C. rw-rw-rw- on **/etc/passwd** and rw-r--r-- on **/etc/shadow**

    D. rw-r--r-- on **/etc/passwd** and rw------- on **/etc/shadow**

57. You have a pre-existing **foobar.service** file that does not have a timer file. Which of the following commands can you use to start **foobar.service** after 90 minutes have elapsed?

    A. systemd-run --on-active="1h 30m" --unit foobar.service

    B. systemctl-run --on-active="1h 30m" --unit foobar.service

    C. system-run --on-active="1h 30m" --unit foobar.service

    D. atd-run --on-active="1h 30m" --unit foobar.service

    E. atdctl --on-active="1h 30m" --unit foobar.service

58. Acting as root, you want to remove all print jobs from the default print queue on your BSD-compatible system. Which of the following commands can you use to accomplish this task?

    A. lprm -f

    B. lprm -a

    C. lprm -r

    D. lprm -

59. You notice that the log files are growing very fast. Which of the following utilities can help you manage these files?

    A. logrotate

    B. rotatelog

    C. sizelog

    D. logsize

60. You want to display information about the current time sources that **chronyd** is accessing. Which of the following commands can help you accomplish this task? Assume you are acting as root.

    A. timesourcectl list

    B. chronyctl list

    C. chronyctl sources

    D. chronyc sources

Practice Exam 4

1. Working with the bash shell, which of the following commands is a valid **for statement**? Select two.

   A. for i in {0..9};do echo $i;done

   B. for((i=0; i<10; i++));do echo $i;done

   C. for(i=0; i<10; i++);do echo $i;done

   D. for i in (0 to 9);do echo $i;done

   E. for i in 0 1 2 3 4 5 6 7 8 9; echo $i; done

2. Which of the following statements about the **~/.xinitrc** file is true?

   A. It is a shell script that is always used to start X automatically when the system boots

   B. It is a shell script that is sourced when using the **startx** command or other programs that call **xinit**

   C. It is a shell script that executes the **startx** command, which is used to start the X window system

   D. It is a shell script that executes the **xinit** command, which is used to start the X window system

   E. It is a shell script that executes the **startx** or **xinit** command (based on the argument passed), both used to start the X window system

3. While working on a Linux system, you notice that the time zone is not configured correctly. How can you solve the problem? Assume you are acting as root.

    A. Delete the current **/etc/localtime** file and replace it with a symbolic link or a copy of the new time zone file chosen within the **/usr/share/zoneinfo** directory

    B. Manually edit the **/etc/localtime** file by entering the time zone you want to use (for example **Europe/Rome**)

    C. Manually edit the **/etc/tzdata** file by entering the time zone you want to use (for example **Europe/Rome**)

    D. Run the **updatetz** command to reconfigure the system time zone

4. You want to send the **foobar** script to the **foo** user as the body of an e-mail. Which of the following commands can you use? Assume that the subject of the e-mail is "**Sending the foobar script**" and the script is located in your current working directory.

    A. mail -s "Sending the foobar script" -r foo < foobar

    B. mail -s "Sending the foobar script" -b foobar -r foo

    C. mail -s "Sending the foobar script" foo < foobar

    D. mail -s "Sending the foobar script" -b foobar foo

5. Which of the following statements about the **/etc/nologin** file is true?

    A. It contains the list of users who are not allowed to log in to the system, each on a separate line

    B. If it exists, all ordinary users are not allowed to log in to the system

    C. If it contains the **false** string, all users are allowed to log in to the system

    D. If it contains the **true** string, all users are allowed to log in to the system

6. You want to run the **foo.sh** script in your home directory at system startup. Which of the following special strings can you use in your **crontab** file to accomplish this task?

    A. @restart

    B. @reboot

    C. @system-up

    D. @startup

7. Which of the following commands can you use to start a stopped printer? And which one can you use to stop a working printer? Assume that your machine uses CUPS printing system.

    A. **cupsenable** and **cupsdisable**

    B. **cupsstart** and **cupsstop**

    C. **spooler-start** and **spooler-stop**

    D. **spenable** and **spdisable**

8. The **/etc/aliases** file on your system contains the following line:

    ```
    root: foo
    ```

    What does it mean? Assume you are acting as root.

    A. All e-mails addressed to the **foo** user on this system are sent to **root**

    B. The local user named **foo** has the same privileges as **root**

    C. All e-mails addressed to **root** on this system are sent to the local user named **foo**

    D. Only the local user named **foo** is allowed to run an interactive shell as **root** by typing the **su** (or **su -**) command without arguments followed by the **root** password

9. Working with bash, you define and export two shell variables: **VAR** with value **a** and **VAR1** with value **b**. What will be the result if you type the **env -u VAR bash - c 'echo $VAR $VAR1'** command?

    A. **a b**

    B. **a**

    C. **b**

    D. An empty line

10. How can you express the 255.255.255.192 netmask using the CIDR notation?

    A. /25

    B. /26

    C. /27

    D. The netmask provided is not valid

11. The ordinary user named **foobar** wants to execute a command with root privileges. Assuming he is allowed to do so, what command can he use to accomplish this task? Write only the command name.

12. Given the following user **crontab** entry:

```
12 11 * * 0 foobar
```

What does the value 12 mean?

    A. The hour

    B. The month

    C. The minutes

    D. The day of the month

13. Which of the following statements about **Toggle Keys** accessibility feature is true?

    A. It is useful for deaf users

    B. It enables users to use the on-screen keyboard

    C. It enables users to use the keyboard's numeric keypad as a pointing device to emulate the mouse

    D. It is useful for users with visual impairments or cognitive disabilities

14. You want to modify the order in which hostname resolution is done. Which of the following lines do you need to edit in **/etc/nsswitch.conf**? Assume you are acting as root.

    A. order

    B. dns

    C. files

    D. hosts

    E. bind

15. Acting as root, you want to remove the job with ID 12 from the destination printer named **Print_office_1**. Which of the following commands can you use? Assume that **Print_office_1** is not the default printer on your BSD-compatible system.

    A. lprm -P Print_office1 -n 12

    B. lprm --id 12 -P Print_office_1

    C. lprm -P Print_office1 12

    D. lprm -n 12 Print_office1

16. You are writing a simple bash script that reads a series of strings from the user within a **for statement** (one string for each cycle - maximum number of cycles 500), and for each string it increments a progressive number **N** starting from zero. Then, at each cycle, the string is checked and if it is equal to the **END** string, the script immediately exits from the loop and prints the final value of **N**. If no **END** string is entered, the script only prints the final value of **N** at the end of the **for** cycle (thus 500). Which of the following commands can you use into the **if-then statement** to immediately exit the loop when the **END** word is entered?

  A. quit

  B. close

  C. break

  D. continue

17. Acting as root, you want to set your hostname permanently. Which of the following files should you edit? Assume that the file is present in your distribution.

  A. /etc/hostname

  B. /etc/hosts

  C. /etc/default/hostcfg

  D. /etc/default/hname

18. Which of the following IPv6 addresses is valid?

  A. 2001::adbc:1423:d0::234

  B. 2001:0:defgh::1423:d0:234

  C. 2001:0:adbc::1423:d0:234:ac0:1

  D. 2001:0:adbc::1423:d0:234

19. Which of the following statements about the Network Time Protocol (NTP) is true? Select two.

    A. It is used to maintain the correct time in a network environment

    B. It is used to correct the time drift of the hardware clock

    C. It is used for a better load balancing in a network environment

    D. It is used to correct the time difference between the system clock and the hardware clock

    E. It is used to correct the time drift of the system clock

20. You want to set the Maximum Transmission Unit (MTU) of the interface eth0 to 5000 bytes. Which of the following commands can you use?

    A. ip addr set dev eth0 mtu 5000

    B. ip link set dev eth0 mtu 5000

    C. ip dev eth0 set mtu 5000

    D. ip iface eth0 set mtu 5000

21. On OpenSSH clients, a system administrator usually maintains a system-wide file that contains the public host keys of all known hosts in the organization to verify the identity of the remote hosts to which a client can connect. What is the name of this file?

    A. /etc/ssh/ssh_known_hosts

    B. ~/.ssh/known_hosts

    C. /etc/ssh_hosts/public_keys

    D. ~/.ssh_hosts/public_keys

    E. /etc/ssh_known_hosts/keys.public

22. Working with bash, you define a shell variable named **VAR** with value **a** and then you type the **VAR=b bash -c 'echo $VAR'** command. What is the value of **VAR** in your bash shell after the execution of this command?

    A. b

    B. a

    C. a b

    D. ab

23. Which of the following statements about the **ifconfig** command is true? Select two.

    A. It is deprecated and has been replaced by the **ipconfig** command

    B. It is a traditional net-tool command used to configure a network interface

    C. If no options and arguments are given, it displays the status of the currently active interfaces

    D. If a single interface is given, it shows the IP address of that interface, but not the hardware address

    E. It can be used to set the network mask and MTU of an interface and to add the default gateway for a machine

24. Acting as root, you want to remove the group named **web_developpers** that you just created (due to a typo). Which of the following commands can you use?

    A. groupdel web_developppers

    B. grpdel web_developppers

    C. grp-del web_developppers

    D. group-del web_developppers

25. Which of the following statements about the **dig** command is true?

    A. It is deprecated and has been replaced by the **nslookup** and **host** commands

    B. It is used only to perform simple tasks, as it shows very few information

    C. It cannot be used to perform reverse lookups (from IP address to hostname)

    D. Its output is normally longer than that of **nslookup** and **host** and is divided into several sections

26. You want to add a new connection using the **nmcli** command. Which of the following connection types (**connection.type** property or **type** alias) is valid? Select two.

    A. ethernet

    B. bluetooth

    C. static

    D. wired

    E. dynamic

27. Acting as root, you want to schedule a new **at job**. Which of the following files should you edit?

    A. /etc/atjobs

    B. /etc/at/atjobs

    C. /etc/jobs/at

    D. No files should be edited

28. You want to test basic connectivity to the host with IP address 192.168.1.100 in your local network. Which of the following commands can help you accomplish this task?

    A. ipck

    B. host

    C. traceroute

    D. ping

29. You want to remotely control a system over a network connection. What can you do?

    A. You can use a RXDCP application

    B. You can use a XRLS application

    C. You can use a VNC application

    D. There is no way to do this

30. You want to look for open ports on your local computer and on other computers within the network. Which of the following auditing tools can you use?

    A. nscan

    B. nmap

    C. portscan

    D. ip-portscan

31. In which user or group management file could you find this entry? Write the full path.

    admin:!:foobar:bar,foo

32. Using systemd as system and service manager, you want to set the system clock to 1st September 2019 at 08:30 am, also updating the RTC time accordingly. Which of the following commands can you use? Assume you are acting as root.

    A. timedatectl set-time "2019-09-01 08:30:00"

    B. timedatectl set-date "2019-09-01 08:30:00"

    C. datetimectl set-time "2019-09-01 08:30:00"

    D. datetimectl set-date "2019-09-01 08:30:00"

33. Using X, which of the following programs can help you extract authorization records from one machine and merge them into another in case of remote logins?

    A. xlog-remote

    B. xremote-auth

    C. xlogin-auth

    D. xauth

34. In Linux **/etc/passwd** is a file of seven colon-delimited fields containing information about users in the system. Which of the following fields can you find in this file?

    A. The user limits

    B. The group identification number of the primary group for the user in the system

    C. The Group Name of the primary group for the user in the system

    D. The expiration date of the user's password

    E. The expiration date of the user account

35. Which of the following statements about the MAC address of an Ethernet card is true?

    A. The MAC address of an Ethernet card is 128-bit long

    B. The MAC address of an Ethernet card is 56-bit long

    C. The MAC address of an Ethernet card is 48-bit long

    D. The MAC address of an Ethernet card is 32-bit long

36. Which of the following statements about the **tzselect** command is true?

    A. It is used to change the current time zone by updating the **/etc/localtime** file based on the value of the **TZ** environment variable

    B. It is used to change the current time zone by updating the **/etc/localtime** file based on the information entered by the user (a series of questions are asked about the current location)

    C. It is used to find out and view the installed time zones

    D. It is used to set the **TZ** environment variable based on the information entered by the user (a series of questions are asked about the current location)

37. Acting as root, you have just updated the **/etc/aliases** file on your system and now you want to rebuild it so that the changes take effect. Which of the following commands can you use to accomplish this task? Assume that you are using sendmail as an MTA on your machine.

    A. sendmail --build-alias

    B. sendmail -bi

    C. sendmail --rebuild-alias

    D. sendmail -br

38. What's the meaning of the following entry in **/etc/rsyslog.conf**?

> *.crit;cron,mail,kern.none /var/log/all.log

    A. All messages with priority **crit**, except cron daemon messages, kernel messages and mail system messages, are logged to **/var/log/all.log**

    B. All messages with priority **crit** or higher, except cron daemon messages, kernel messages and mail system messages, are logged to **/var/log/all.log**

    C. All messages with priority **crit** or lower, except cron daemon messages, kernel messages and mail system messages, are logged to **/var/log/all.log**

    D. All cron daemon messages, kernel messages and mail system messages with priority **crit** or higher are logged to **/var/log/all.log**

39. Acting as root, you want to see which processes are currently using network port 21 on your system. Which of the following commands can you use?

    A. pstrace -v 21/tcp

    B. pstrace -v tcp 21

    C. fuser -v 21/tcp

    D. fuser -v tcp 21

40. What can you use as a **cron** replacement to run tasks on a regular basis on machines that use systemd as system and service manager?

    A. batch

    B. systemd journal

    C. systemd timers

    D. at

41. Working with the bash shell, you want to test if the **report.txt** file exists and is a symbolic link. Which of the following commands can you use?

    A. [-L report.txt] && echo "It's a symbolic link" || echo "Not a symbolic link"

    B. [-s report.txt] && echo "It's a symbolic link" || echo "Not a symbolic link"

    C. [-S report.txt] && echo "It's a symbolic link" || echo "Not a symbolic link"

    D. [-f report.txt] && echo "It's a symbolic link" || echo "Not a symbolic link"

42. The **foobar** user wants to add his private key **/home/foobar/.ssh/id_rsa** to the SSH authentication agent. Which of the following commands can he use?

    A. ssh-add

    B. ssh-addkey

    C. add-key

    D. key-add

    E. ssh-keygen

43. You want to add a new user account, also creating its home directory. Which of the following options of the **useradd** command can you use? Assume that you are acting as root and that **CREATE_HOME** in **/etc/login.defs** is set to no.

    A. --add-home

    B. -M

    C. -m

    D. --home-add

44. Acting as root, you want to set access restrictions to your NTP server. Which directive should you use in **/etc/ntp.conf** to accomplish this task? Write only the directive name.

45. Which of the following facilities can you use in the **rsyslog** main configuration file? Select two.

    A. mail

    B. user

    C. users

    D. daemon-msg

    E. printer

46. Working with the bash shell, you want to test if the **fooscript.sh** file exists and is executable. Which of the following commands can you use?

    A. [-w fooscript.sh] && echo "It's executable" || echo "Not executable"

    B. test -r fooscript.sh && echo "It's executable" || echo "Not executable"

    C. [-x fooscript.sh] && echo "It's executable" || echo "Not executable"

    D. test -e fooscript.sh && echo "It's executable" || echo "Not executable"

47. Which of the following directives can you find in a **logrotate** configuration file? Select two.

    A. log-size

    B. dateext

    C. rotate

    D. counter

    E. log-period

    F. size-max

48. DNS resolution doesn't seem to work within your network, but you need to print the kernel routing table. Which of the following options of the **route** command can help you in this situation only show IP addresses instead of trying to determine the associated hostnames?

    A. -i

    B. -n

    C. -d

    D. -a

49. Acting as root, you want to prevent the user account named **foobar** from logging into the system. What can you do? Assume that **foobar** is a system user account, created on your machine only to run a specific task.

    A. Add the **foobar** user to the **nologin** group

    B. Create the **/etc/nologin** file, writing **foobar** on the first line. If this file already exists, just add **foobar** on a new line.

    C. Change the default shell of **foobar** to **/bin/false**

    D. Run the **nologinuser foobar** command

50. You want to configure whether journal log data should be compressed before it is written to the file system. Which of the following files should you edit? Assume you are acting as root.

    A. /etc/system/journal.conf

    B. /etc/journal/systemd.conf

    C. /etc/systemd/journald.conf

    D. /etc/journald/system.conf

51. The eth0 device has two connection profiles: one for DHCP addressing called **dhcp-conn** (the main profile that is normally used) and one for static IP addressing called **static-conn** (a profile for a specific network that uses only static IP addressing). The **dhcp-conn** connection profile is currently up, but you want to switch to the **static-conn** connection profile to work on the specific network with only static IP addressing. Which of the following commands can you use? Assume that your system uses NetworkManager.

    A. nmcli disable-conn dhcp-conn;nmcli enable-conn static-conn

    B. nmcli connection switch static-conn dhcp-conn

    C. nmcli connection switch dhcp-conn static-conn

    D. nmcli connection down dhcp-conn;nmcli connection up static-conn

52. Given the following bash extract:

```
# foo=bar
# echo $foo
bar
# alias foovalue='echo The value of foo is $foo'
# foo=foobar
```

What is the result if you type **foovalue** in the bash shell? Assume you are acting as root.

    A. The value of foo is foobar

    B. The value of foo is bar

    C. The value of foo is $foo

    D. echo The value of foo is $foo

    E. An error: the **alias** command cannot be used with shell variables

53. You are sick of having to type the GPG passphrase every time you decrypt a document using your private key. Which of the following programs, which stores GPG private keys and their passphrase, can help you so that you are asked for the passphrase only once at the beginning and not every time you decrypt a document?

    A. session-gpgkey

    B. gpg-agent

    C. gpg-keyring

    D. session-store

54. You want to edit the **/etc/hosts.allow** file so that only address 192.168.1.100 can access all services. Which of the following lines should you put in this file? Assume that you are controlling access via TCP wrappers.

    A. ALL: ALL

    B. ALL: 192.168.1.100

    C. 192.168.1.100 *

    D. * 192.168.1.100

55. Working with bash, you defined a custom function named **foobar**, but you do not remember exactly all of its instructions. Which of the following commands can help you look at this function, also displaying all shell variables and other defined functions?

    A. set

    B. show_function

    C. show

    D. set_function

56. Which of the following network masks corresponds to the CIDR notation /25?

    A. 255.255.255.192

    B. 255.255.255.128

    C. 255.255.255.224

    D. 255.255.255.240

    E. 255.255.255.254

57. You want to change the current system time zone. Which of the following commands can you use? Assume that you are acting as root and that your Linux system uses systemd as system and service manager.

    A. timectl

    B. timedatectl

    C. datectl

    D. timezonectl

58. You are using a Linux system with shadow passwords. Which of the following statements is true?

    A. Encrypted passwords for users and groups are stored in **/etc/passwd** and **/etc/group**

    B. Encrypted passwords for users and groups are stored in **/etc/passwd** and **/etc/shadow**

    C. Encrypted passwords for users and groups are stored in **/etc/gshadow** and **/etc/group**

    D. Encrypted passwords for users and groups are stored in **/etc/shadow** and **/etc/gshadow**

59. Which of the following statements about X11 forwarding in SSH is true?

    A. To use it, you need to invoke **ssh** with the **-x** option

    B. To use it, you need to invoke **ssh** with the **--X11Forward** option

    C. If X11 forwarding is in effect, the **FORWARD_TO** variable is automatically set in the shell of the remote host

    D. If X11 forwarding is in effect, the **DISPLAY** variable is automatically set in the shell of the remote host

60. In Linux, **nmcli** is a command-line tool that operates on a series of objects. Which of the following is valid? Select two.

    A. connection

    B. networking

    C. network

    D. access

    E. interface

Answers

Answers to the Practice Exam 1

1. D - Topic 105.2

Working with the bash shell, you can use positional parameters to process command line arguments of a bash script. Parameter **0** refers to the name of the shell script, parameter **1** refers to the first command line argument, parameter **2** refers to the second command line argument and so on. If you have more than nine parameters, you must save or process the first parameter and then drop it using the **shift** command so that the second parameter becomes the first, the third parameter becomes the second and so on. Within a script, you can reference these parameters by using the **$** symbol, as with shell variables. Therefore, you can use **echo $1 $3** inside your **foo.sh** script to print the first and third variables passed to the script, making option D the correct answer. For completeness, option A prints the name of the script and the second variable passed to the script, option B prints the name of the script followed by the **,2** string and option C prints the first variable passed to the script followed by the **,3** string.

2. C - Topic 106.1

In Linux, **xhost** is a server access control program for the X server. In particular, it is used to add and delete user names or host names to the list allowed to make connections to the X server (in this case X.org-X11). You can use the **xhost [+]name** command to add the specified name (host name or user name) to the list allowed to connect to the X server (the plus sign is optional), and the **xhost - name** command to remove the specified name (host name or user name) from the list of allowed to connect to the X server (existing connections are not broken, but new connection attempts will be denied). Likewise, to add a particular IP address to your access control list, you can run **xhost +IPaddress** or **xhost**

IPaddress, while to remove it, you can run **xhost -IPaddress**. Therefore, option C is the correct answer. For completeness, option B specifies that access is granted to everyone (access control is turned off), option A has a wrong syntax, and options D and E contain invalid commands.

3. **192.168.7.255 - Topic 109.1**

In the CIDR notation, /22 corresponds to a network mask of 255.255.252.0 (the first 22 bits are set to 1). To calculate the broadcast address, you can put in binary form the network address (11000000.10101000.00000100.00000000) and the network mask (11111111.11111111.11111100.00000000), and then set the network address bits to 1 when the corresponding bits of the network mask are 0 (thus the last 10 bits, 32-22=10). Therefore, the broadcast address is 11000000.10101000.00000111.11111111, or in decimal form 192.168.7.255.

4. **A - Topic 107.1**

The **usermod** command is used to modify a user account. In particular, the **-l** option of this command followed by a new login name is used to change the old login name of the specified user account by replacing it with the new one. This makes option A the correct answer. For completeness, option B reverses the new and old login name, while options C and D specify an incorrect long option for **usermod** (the correct one is **--login**). Note that **usermod -l** only changes the name of the user account; therefore, the user's home directory name should probably be changed manually to reflect the change.

5. **B, D - Topic 107.1**

In Linux, you can lock a user account using the **usermod -L** (**usermod --lock**) and **passwd -l** commands, and you can unlock a user account using the **usermod -U** (**usermod --unlock**) and **passwd -u** commands. This makes options B and D the correct answers. Remember that when a user account is locked, an exclamation mark (!) is put in front of the encrypted password of the user, and when it is unlocked, the exclamation mark is removed. For completeness, the **chage** command is used to change the user password expiry information and does not have the **-u** and **-U** options, while the **unlock** command does not exist.

6. B - Topic 109.3

The **ip** command is used to show and manipulate routing, devices, policy routing and tunnels. In particular, you can assign an IP address to a specific interface on the fly using the **ip address add** command or, in abbreviated form, **ip addr add** or **ip a add** (the **address** object identifies the IPv4 or IPv6 address on a device). Therefore, option B is the correct answer. For completeness, the **ip link set** command changes the device attributes (the **link** object identifies a network device), the **address** object does not have the **set** command, and finally the **link** object does not have the **address** command.

7. C - Topic 110.2

The **disable** attribute is used within a specific service configuration file managed by **xinetd** to specify whether the service is disabled or enabled. In particular, you can use **disable = yes** or **disable = no** to disable or enable the service. This makes option C the correct answer. For completeness, the **enable**, **active**, and **inactive** attributes are invalid.

8. E - Topic 105.2

As described in the question, you define two shell variables (**FOO** with value **Hello** and **BAR** with value **World**), but you do not export them. Therefore, **FOO** and **BAR** remain available only in the current working shell and not in child processes such as shell scripts. As a result, when you launch the **hello.sh** script, it runs in a new shell instance and does not inherit these two variables. Then an empty line is printed, making option E the correct answer.

9. B - Topic 105.1

The **unset** command is used to remove variable or function names. If no options are supplied, or the **-v** option is given, each name specified on the command line refers to a shell variable. Therefore, you can remove multiple variables with a single **unset** command, making option B the correct answer. For completeness, the **remove** command does not exist.

10.C - Topic 107.2

Each line in a **user crontab file** contains six fields separated by a space: the **minutes of the hour** (0 - 59), the **hour of the day** (0 - 23), the **day of the month** (1 - 31), the **month of the year** (1 - 12), the **day of the week** (0 - 7 with Sunday 0 or 7), and the **command to run**. Therefore, option C contains the right **crontab** entry to run the script every day at 01:00 am. For completeness, option A runs the script every Sunday at 01:00 am, option B runs the script every day at 00:01 am, and option D runs the script every Sunday at 00:01 am.

11.A - Topic 107.3

In Linux, you can set **LANG=C** at the beginning of a script to disable localization (therefore, the output of the script is not passed through **locale translations**). This makes option A the correct answer. Remember that **LANG** is the environment variable normally used to specify a **locale**.

12.A - Topic 107.2

The **/etc/at.allow** and **/etc/at.deny** files determine which user can submit commands for later execution via **at** or **batch**. In particular, they consist of a list of usernames, each on a separate line. This makes option A the correct answer.

13.D - Topic 105.1

When **root** types the **su foobar** command, it only switches the user, keeping the environment from the **root** original login session. As a result, the current working directory is not changed (it is still **/root**) and therefore, when the **ls -l** command is executed, a permission denied message is displayed (**foobar** cannot list files in the **/root** directory). This makes option D the correct answer.

14.A, D - Topic 107.1

As specified in the question, **/etc/shadow** is a file of nine colon-delimited fields that contains encrypted passwords of the users. Each line describes a single user and contains the following fields: **Username** (the user's login name), **Encrypted**

Password, **Date of Last Password Change**, **Minimum Password Age** (the minimum number of days after a password change that the user will have to wait before being allowed to change the password again), **Maximum Password Age** (the maximum number of days the password is valid after which the user must change his password before being able to use his account), **Password Warning Period** (the number of days before a password is going to expire during which the user should be warned that the password must be changed), **Password Inactivity Period** (the number of days after a password has expired during which the user should update the password, otherwise the account will be disabled), **Account Expiration Date** and a **reserved field**. Therefore, options A and D are the correct answers.

15. C - Topic 109.2

In Linux, **/etc/hosts** is a simple text file that holds mappings of IP addresses to hostnames on a single computer (one line per IP address). Therefore, if you need to resolve a handful of hostnames in a small network without configuring a DNS server, you need to keep this file up to date on individual computers, making option C the correct answer. For completeness, **/etc/hostname** holds the computer's default hostname (not all systems use this file), **/etc/resolv.conf** holds the main information on name resolution (it is the resolver configuration file), and **/etc/host-mapping** does not exist.

16. D - Topic 109.1

In the CIDR notation, /29 corresponds to a network mask of 255.255.255.248 and so the network address and the network mask are consistent. The last three bits (32-29=3) can be used for network hosts within your network: as a result, you have six IP addresses to assign to your network hosts (2^3 - broadcast address - network address = 6), making option D the correct answer.

17. D - Topic 108.2

In Linux, the **journalctl** command is used to query the contents of the systemd journal. In particular, if invoked without parameters, it shows the entire contents of the journal starting from the oldest entry, while if one or more match arguments are specified, the output is filtered accordingly. Therefore, option D is the correct answer.

18.D - Topic 109.1

The network mask is used to find out which part of an IP address is the network address and which is the host address. In particular, if the network mask is expressed in binary form, the set of binary values 1 represents the network address, while the set of binary values 0 represents the host address. The network mask 255.255.255.200 can be expressed in binary form as 11111111.11111111.11111111.11001000 and, as you can see, you do not have a separation between binary values 1 and 0. Therefore, the network mask is not valid, making option D the correct answer.

19.D - Topic 109.3

The **traceroute** command is used to print the route that a packet takes to reach a specific network host and can be useful in identifying where there may be a problem between source and destination. This makes option D the correct answer. For completeness, **ping** is a network utility to test if a host is reachable, **host** is a simple utility for performing DNS lookups, and **hostpath** does not exist.

20.A - Topic 109.4

In Linux, **/etc/nsswitch.conf** is the name service switch configuration file, which can be used to specify the order in which hostnames are resolved. In particular, you can modify the **hosts** line to specify to the system what to consult first. In the question, first you find **files** which stands for **/etc/hosts**, and then **dns** which stands for DNS servers. Therefore, the **/etc/hosts** file is consulted first for name resolution, making option A the correct answer.

21.iconv - Topic 107.3

The **iconv** command is used to convert the encoding of characters of a specified file (or standard input if no file is given) from one coded character set to another.

22.C - Topic 107.3

The **/usr/share/zoneinfo** directory contains time zone data files, and in modern Linux systems, **/etc/localtime** is a symbolic link to one of these files. Therefore, option C is the correct answer.

23.C - Topic 109.3

When working as a system administrator, it can often happen to troubleshoot networking issues on client hosts. Most of the time these problems are related to DNS server malfunctions, making option C the correct answer. The other problems, described in options A, B and D are possible, but not very likely. As a tip, when a network problem occurs on a client host, always remember to first check that the machine has network connectivity, a valid IP address, and correct IP addresses (even in the right order) of the DNS servers.

24.B - Topic 110.3

In Linux, **gpg** is a useful tool that provides digital encryption and signing services using the OpenPGP standard. In particular, the **--gen-key** option of this command generates GPG keys, saving them in a keyring in the **~/.gnupg** directory. Therefore, option B is the correct answer.

25.A - Topic 110.1

The SUID and SGID programs are potentially risky because they are executed as the owner or group of the program file instead of the user who runs them. The risk increases if the owner and/or group of the program file is root. In fact, by running these programs, a user could perform potentially harmful actions. For this reason, a good administrator should periodically check the system to find the SUID and SGID programs and possibly change their permissions if not set correctly. To achieve this goal, you can use the **find** command with the **-perm** option. In particular, the expressions **-perm +4000**, **-perm +2000**, and **-perm +6000** tell **find** to search respectively for files with only the SUID bit set, with only the SGID bit set, and with the SUID or SGID bits set. You can restrict the search to regular files by adding the **-type f** expression. Therefore, option A is the correct answer. For completeness, the **find** command does not have the **-suid**, **-sgid**, and **-auth** options. Finally, remember that **-perm +PermissionMode** is an old way of searching for files with any of the specified permission bits set, which has been deprecated in **findutils-4.2.21** in favor of **-perm /PermissionMode**.

26. B, C - Topic 109.1

The address 192.200.100.224 can be expressed in binary form as 11000000.11001000.01100100.11100000 and the CIDR notation /29 corresponds to a network mask of 11111111.11111111.11111111.11111000 (255.255.255.248). The network address and the network mask are consistent and the last three bits (32-29=3) can be used for network hosts. Therefore, the IP addresses 192.200.100.225 (11000000.11001000.01100100.11100001) and 192.200.100.230 (11000000.11001000.01100100.11100110) can be used for hosts within the specified network, making options B and C the correct answers. For completeness, the IP address 192.200.100.224 represents the network address (it corresponds to 11000000.11001000.01100100.11100000), the IP address 192.200.100.231 represents the broadcast address (it corresponds to 11000000.11001000.01100100.11100111), and the IP address 192.200.100.248 cannot be used for hosts within the network indicated in the question (it corresponds to 11000000.11001000.01100100.11111000).

27. C - Topic 109.3

In Linux, **ping** is a useful network utility for testing basic connectivity between two hosts. In particular, it sends **ICMP ECHO_REQUEST** packets to a network host to test if it is reachable and the **-c** option of this command determines the number of packets to send. This makes option C the correct answer. For completeness, the **-n** option is used to not attempt to find the hostnames associated with IP addresses (numeric output only), while the **-C** and **-N** options do not exist.

28. A - Topic 106.1

In Linux, **~/.xsession-errors** is the file where you can look to find out all the errors, logged by the X Window system, that occur within your graphical environment. This makes option A the correct answer. Since all the graphical applications running on your machine log error messages in **~/.xsession-errors**, this file can grow very fast. Therefore, rememeber to pay attention to its size.

29.C - Topic 109.2

The **ifup** and **ifdown** commands are used to activate and deactivate a network interface respectively, based on the interface definitions in the specific configuration file of the distribution you are using. This makes option C the correct answer. For completeness, the **iface** and **ifdisable** commands do not exist.

30.A - Topic 105.2

The **seq** command is used to print a sequence of numbers. In particular, the **seq -s: 5 3 10** command specifies to print numbers from 5 to 10, in steps of 3. The **-s** option tells **seq** to separate numbers with colons. Therefore, option A is the correct answer.

31.unalias rm - Topic 105.1

As described in answer 7 of the Assessment Test, an alias is usually used to define new command names that are easy to remember, create command shortcuts that avoid typing long commands, and implement some command options as a default. For example, the **alias rm="rm -i"** command implements a new alias for **rm** so that each time you type **rm** at the command line it runs in interactive mode preventing the accidental deletion of files. If you want to remove an alias from the list of defined aliases, you can use the **unalias** command specifying the name of the alias to remove. Therefore, the right command to use is **unalias rm**.

32.B - Topic 107.1

In Linux, **/etc/passwd** is a file of seven colon-delimited fields that contains information about users. Each line describes a single user and contains the following fields: **Username** (the user's login name), **Password** (the encrypted password or an **x** if shadow passwords are used), **User ID** (UID - the User

Identification Number in the system), **Group ID** (GID - the Group Identification Number of the primary group of the user in the system), **GECOS** (an optional comment field), **Home Directory** (the absolute path of the user's home directory) and **Shell** (the absolute path of the program to run at login, which is usually the user's shell). Therefore, option B is the correct answer.

33. A - Topic 108.1

The **date** command is used to print or set the system date and time. In particular, you can set the date and time simply by using **date** followed by the date and time you want to set, according to the following format **MMDDhhmm[[CC]YY][.ss]**. As a result, option A is the correct answer. Note that the year, expressed using only the last two digits or the four digits with the century, is optional (if not indicated, it means the current year) as well as the seconds (if not indicated, it means 00). For completeness, the **date** command also has a **-s** option, which is used to set the system clock to the date and time specified by a string.

34. C - Topic 109.2

In Linux, **nmcli** is a command-line tool for controlling NetworkManager and reporting network status. In particular, you can use the **nmcli connection show** command to list all connection profiles (in general the **connection** object is used to start, stop, and manage network connections). This command is equivalent to **nmcli con show** and **nmcli c s**, making option C the correct answer. For completeness, the other options specify invalid objects.

35. B - Topic 105.2

The **case** construct is used to simplify conditional statements (**if-then-else statements**). In particular, it can be useful when you have a list of possibilities, each of which has a matching value, and you want to perform a particular action for each of these values (thus for each possibility). Therefore, option B is the correct answer. For completeness, **for** and **while** are looping constructs that execute a series of commands zero or more times, while **seq** is a command used to print a sequence of numbers.

36. A, D - Topic 108.3

In Linux, a MTA, which stands for Mail Transfer Agent, is used to deliver e-mails between users and between systems. The most popular MTAs are **sendmail**, **postfix**, and **exim**. Therefore, options A and D are the correct answers.

37. C, E - Topic 108.1

The **hwclock** command is used to query and set the hardware clock. In particular, you can display the current value of the hardware clock using the **hwclock** command without any option, synchronize the system clock from the hardware clock using the **--hctosys** or **-s** option, and synchronize the hardware clock from the system clock using the **--systohc** or **-w** option. Therefore, options C and E are the correct answers. For completeness, the **-z** and **--setsys** options are invalid.

38. D - Topic 110.2

In Linux, the **/etc/nologin** file prevents ordinary users from logging into the system. In particular, if this file exists and is readable, only root may log into the system; ordinary users are shown the contents of this file and their logins are refused. Therefore, as root you can create **/etc/nologin** to perform, for example, maintenance tasks, thus preventing system logins by ordinary users. This makes option D the correct answer.

39. C, E - Topic 109.2

In Linux, **nmcli** is a useful command-line tool used to control NetworkManager and report network status. In particular, it can perform many operations, depending on the type of object on which it operates. You can use the following objects: **general** to show NetworkManager status and permissions, get and change the system hostname, as well as NetworkManager logging level and domains, **networking** to query NetworkManager networking status, and enable/disable networking, **radio** to show radio switches status, or enable/disable the switches, **connection** to start, stop and manage network connections, **device** to show and manage network interfaces, **agent** to run **nmcli** as a NetworkManager secret agent, or polkit agent, and **monitor** to observe

NetworkManager activity and look at changes in connectivity status, devices or connection profiles. Therefore, options C and E are the correct answers.

40.C - Topic 108.3

As an ordinary user, you can forward all your incoming e-mails by editing the **.forward** file in your home directory or creating a new one if it doesn't exist. In this file you only need to specify a user on the same or another machine or an e-mail address or a file name or a program to pipe to. You can also separate multiple entries with a comma or a new line. The **|~/bar** line, specified in the **.forward** file of the question, has a leading vertical bar character, which indicates the pipe and so all the incoming e-mails (not only those marked as spam) are piped to the **~/bar** program, making option C the correct answer.

41.C - Topic 105.1

When bash is invoked as an interactive login shell, or as a non-interactive shell with the **--login** option, it first reads and executes commands from the **/etc/profile** file, if that file exists (along with any **.sh** files in **/etc/profile.d**). Then it checks the home directory for the **~/.bash_profile**, **~/.bash_login**, and **~/.profile** files, in that order, and runs the first one that it finds. This makes option C the correct answer.

42.D - Topic 108.1

Option D describes exactly what happens when there are multiple **server** entries in **/etc/ntp.conf**. In fact, the system polls all the specified servers, but uses the one that provides the cleanest time data.

43.D - Topic 107.2

The **crontab** command is used to maintain **crontab files** for individual users. In particular, the **-e** option of this command edits the current **crontab** using the editor specified by the **VISUAL** or **EDITOR** environment variables. Therefore, option D is the correct answer. In Linux, each user can have their own **crontab**

file, and although these files are located in **/var/spool/**, they are not intended to be edited directly. For completeness, **cronedit** and **crontabs** do not exist.

44. B - Topic 108.2

The **systemd-cat** command is used to connect the standard input and output of a process to the journal or as a filtering tool in a shell pipeline to pass the output generated by the previous pipeline element to the journal. If no parameter is passed, **systemd-cat** writes everything it reads from standard input to the journal, while if parameters are passed, they are executed as command line with standard output and standard error connected to the journal. This makes option B the correct answer.

45. D - Topic 106.3

Option D describes exactly the purpose of the **Sticky Keys** accessibility feature and is therefore the correct answer. In fact, it was designed for people who have difficulty pressing multiple keys simultaneously. When enabled, the modifier key pressed (CTRL, ALT, or SHIFT) remains active until another key is pressed. For completeness, options A, B and C describe the purpose of the **Bounces Keys**, **Mouse Keys**, and **Slow Keys** accessibility features, respectively.

46. B - Topic 106.2

XDMCP, which stands for X Display Manager Control Protocol, is a network protocol that handles local GUI logins as well as remote GUI logins. In Linux, there are several XDMCP servers (for example XDM, KDM, GDM/GDM3, and LightDM), whose purpose is to start X and control access to X via a login prompt and then start and prepare the desktop environment for the user. Therefore, option B is the correct answer.

47. B - Topic 110.1

The **/etc/sudoers** file determines the users' **sudo** privileges on the system, specifying which tasks different users can perform using the **sudo** command (who may run what). This makes option B the correct answer.

48. B, C, E - Topic 108.2

In **/etc/rsyslog.conf**, a **facility** is the subsystem that generates a specific log message. For example, some possible values are: **kern** for kernel messages, **mail** for mail system messages, **cron** for cron messages, and **local0** through **local7** for locally defined application messages. This makes options B, C and E the correct answers. For completeness, **notice** is a type of priority, while **local10** is not a valid facility.

49. /etc/ssh/sshd_config - Topic 110.3

In Linux, **/etc/ssh/sshd_config** is the OpenSSH server configuration file. Therefore, you can edit this file to change the port number on which the server is listening, as well as all the other options of your OpenSSH server.

50. B - Topic 108.2

In Linux, **/etc/rsyslog.conf** is the main configuration file for **rsyslog**. The syntax for each line in this file is as follows: **facility.priority action**, where **facility** is the subsystem that generates a specific log message, **priority** is the importance of the message, and **action** is the file (or other location) in which to save log messages. If this syntax is used, all messages of the given **facility** with the specified level of **priority** or higher are logged. If the **priority** is preceded with an equal sign, only the messages with the specified **priority** are logged, and if the **priority** is preceded with an exclamation mark, the meaning of the match is reversed. Therefore, option B is the correct answer. For completeness, option A only logs e-mail log messages with priority **info**, while options C and D have a wrong syntax.

51. B - Topic 108.4

In Linux, the **lpr** command is used to print files. In particular, you can specify a printer name with the **-P** option, otherwise the default printer is used. This makes option B the correct answer. For completeness, the **-p** option is used to specify that the print file should be formatted with a shaded header with the date, time, job name, and page number, the **-r** option is used to specify that the print file should be deleted after submitting it, and the **--printer-name** option does not exist.

52. B - Topic 108.4

In Linux, **cupsd.conf** is the main configuration file for **CUPS**, while **printers.conf** is the printer configuration file that defines the local printers that are available (both files are normally located in the **/etc/cups** directory). Therefore, option B is the correct answer.

53. B, C - Topic 107.1

The **id** and **groups** commands are used to print user and group information and group membership for the specified user account, respectively. This makes options B and C the correct answers.

54. B - Topic 109.4

In Linux, **host** is a simple utility used to perform DNS lookups, converting names to IP addresses and vice versa. This makes option B the correct answer. For completeness, other utilities that perform these translations are **dig** and **nslookup**, although the latter has been deprecated.

55. A - Topic 108.3

In Linux, **/etc/aliases** (or sometimes **/etc/mail/aliases**) is the mail alias file, where you can define one or more destinations for all the incoming e-mails of a specified username. Once added a new mail alias, the **newaliases** command must be run to compile and rebuild the mail alias file, making option A the correct answer.

56. B - Topic 107.2

In systemd, timer units can be used as an alternative to **cron** to schedule Linux jobs. In particular, the **OnCalendar** events specify the date and time when jobs are executed and use the following syntax: **DayOfWeek** (optional) **Year-Month-Day Hour:Minute:Second**. Therefore, option B is the correct answer. For completeness, remember that the asterisk operator (*) means any value.

57. C - Topic 110.2

In Linux,**/etc/hosts.allow** and **/etc/hosts.deny** are access control files used by TCP Wrappers to determine whether or not a machine is allowed to connect to a specific service. Therefore, option C is the correct answer. For completeness, the **xinetd** super daemon restricts access to specific services without using **TCP Wrappers,** while **initx** and **xconn** do not exist.

58. B - Topic 110.3

When GPG keys are generated, a private key and a public key are created. As the names imply, the private key must remain private and must never be exchanged, while the public key can be made available to everyone. Therefore, you can encrypt a file with the public key of another user, who can decrypt it using the corresponding private key (which only he must have). Furthermore, you can sign a file using your private key and other users, who have your public key, can verify the signature. This makes option B the correct answer.

59. C - Topic 110.3

The **ssh-keygen** command is used to generate, manage and convert authentication keys for SSH. This makes option C the correct answer.

60. C - Topic 110.1

The **last** command looks through the file named **/var/log/wtmp** and displays information about all logins and logouts on a Linux system since that file was created. Therefore, option C is the correct answer. Remember that **wtmp** could be rotated; so if you need to see an older version of this file, you can use the **last -f** command followed by the name of the file you want to read (for example **/var/log/wtmp.1)**.

Answers to the Practice Exam 2

1. **A - Topic 105.2**

   Shell variables are only available in the current working shell. If you want to make a shell variable visible (thus usable) in a child process (such as a shell script), you must export it. Therefore, when you launch your **hello.sh** script, it runs in a new shell instance and inherits the value of the exported environment variables **FOO** and **BAR**. As a result, the script prints the **Hello World** string, making option C the correct answer.

2. **/etc/ssh/ssh_config - Topic 110.3**

   In Linux, **/etc/ssh/ssh_config** is the system-wide configuration file for OpenSSH clients. In particular, it provides defaults for those values that are not indicated in the user-specific configuration file, and for those users who do not have a configuration file. Therefore, assuming that no user has their own ssh configuration file, and that, acting as root, you maintain a global configuration file for all users of a machine, you can edit **/etc/ssh/ssh_config** to change the port number to connect to the remote OpenSSH server. For completeness, remember that a ssh client program receives its configuration from the command-line options, from the user-specific configuration file (**~/.ssh/config**), and from the system-wide configuration file (**/etc/ssh/ssh_config**), just in this order (the first value obtained for each configuration parameter is used).

3. **A - Topic 108.2**

   Option A contains the right syntax for sending all mail log messages with only priority **info** to **/var/log/mail.log** and is therefore the correct answer. For completeness, option B logs messages with priority **info** or higher and options C and D have a wrong syntax. Refer to answer 50 of Practice Exam 1 for a detailed description of the basic configuration of **/etc/rsyslog.conf** and for the correct syntax to use.

4. B, D - Topic 109.1

The addresses reserved for private use range from 10.0.0.0 to 10.255.255.255 for class A networks (1.0.0.0 - 127.255.255.255), from 172.16.0.0 to 172.31.255.255 for class B networks (128.0.0.0 - 191.255.255.255), and from 192.168.0.0 to 192.168.255.255 for class C networks (192.0.0.0 - 223.255.255.255). Therefore, options B and D are the correct answers.

5. C - Topic 105.1

Once you have logged into the bash shell, you can start other shells to run your commands. If a shell accepts commands from the keyboard, it is an interactive shell (the user can interact with the shell), otherwise it is a non-interactive shell (it's often run from a script - no interaction between the shell and the user). When an interactive shell that is not a login shell is started, bash reads and executes commands from the **~/.bashrc** script, if that file exists. Therefore, option C is the correct answer.

6. B - Topic 107.3

The **locale** command invoked without arguments is used to write information about the current **locale environment**. Therefore, option B is the correct answer.

7. B - Topic 109.2

The question shows the output of the **ip route list** command, which is used to display the kernel routing table on a Linux system. An outgoing packet is transmitted to the default gateway (192.168.5.1) when no other route specification matches the destination IP address of the packet (default route) and, without it, you can only communicate with the machines on your local network (192.168.5.0). In fact, an outgoing packet to a host in the local network (for example the host with IP address 192.168.5.100) is transmitted directly to the destination over the network interface eth0. Therefore, option B is the correct answer.

8. C - Topic 107.2

The **/etc/cron.allow** and **/etc/cron.deny** files determine which user can access **cron**. In particular, they consist of a list of usernames, each on a separate line. Therefore, option C is the correct answer.

9. A - Topic 108.3

In Linux, the **mailq** command is used to display a summary of the mail messages queued for future delivery, making option A the correct answer. For completeness, remember that this command is equivalent to **sendmail -bp**.

10. A, D - Topic 108.1

The **hwclock** command is used to query and set the hardware clock. In particular, the **--systohc** (or **-w**) option of this command is used to synchronize the hardware clock from the system clock, while the **--hctosys** (or **-s**) option is used to synchronize the system clock from the hardware clock. This makes options A and D the correct answers. For completeness, the **--syshc** and **-t** options do not exist for the **hwclock** command.

11. C - Topic 105.1

The **useradd** command is used to create a new user or to update default new user information. The **-m** option of this command creates the user's home directory if it does not exist, and the files and directories contained in the skeleton directory are copied to the home directory of this new user. You can specify a custom skeleton directory with the **-k** option of the **useradd** command, and if this option is not used, the skeleton directory is defined by the **SKEL** variable in **/etc/default/useradd** or, by default, **/etc/skel**. Therefore, option C is the correct answer.

12.A - Topic 105.2

The **let** built-in command is used to evaluate an arithmetic expression and assign its value to a variable. You don't need to use **$** before the variable name, making option A correct and option B incorrect. For completeness, option C defines a variable named **VAR** with value **10+5** (string), while option D makes the **VAR** variable visible to subshells after assigning it the value **10+5** (string).

13.C - Topic 107.3

A **locale** is a set of environment variables that defines the user's language, country and character set encoding as well as other special preferences. The **LANG** environment variable is normally used to specify a **locale** on a Linux system and takes the following form: **language_territory.codeset[@modifier]**, where **language** is the language code, **territory** is the country code, **codeset** is the character set or the encoding identifier, and **modifier** is a locale-specific code that modifies the default behavior. Therefore, **it_IT.UTF-8** is a valid value for **LANG** (Italian language - country Italy - UTF-8 encoding), making option C the correct answer.

14.B - Topic 108.1

As described in answer 5 of the Assessment Test, the **server** directive in **/etc/chrony.conf** specifies an NTP server (by name or IP address), which can be used as a time source. This directive supports many options among which one of the most important is **iburst** that is used to allow **chronyd** to make the first update of the clock shortly after startup, in order to speed up the initial synchronization (the interval between the first four requests sent to the NTP server will be 2 seconds or less instead of the interval specified by the **minpoll** option). This makes option B the correct answer. For completeness, the **speed**, **quick-sync**, **fastsync**, and **driftstart** options do not exist for the **server** directive.

15.C - Topic 107.2

The entry in the question refers to a **user crontab file** and specifies the time to run the **foobar** job. In particular, the asterisk operator (*) means any value and the comma operator (,) is the value list separator. Therefore, **foobar** runs at 11:10 am on Sunday and Monday, making option C the correct answer. Refer to answer 10 of Practice Exam 1 for a detailed description of all fields in a **user crontab file**.

16. B, C - Topic 110.2

The **bind** or **interface** attribute is used within a specific service configuration file managed by **xinetd** to bind the service to one IP address on the system. Therefore, options B and C are the correct answers. For completeness, the **only_from** attribute specifies the remote hosts to which the service is available, while the **inet_addr** and **iface** attributes are invalid.

17. D - Topic 108.2

In Linux, the **journalctl** command is used to query the systemd journal. In particular, the **--since=** and **--until=** options filter entries by date (the first shows entries on or newer than the specified date and the second shows entries on or older than the specified date), the **-p** (**--priority**) option filters entries by message priorities or priority range, and the **-r** (**--reverse**) option reverses the output so that the newest entries are displayed first. Therefore, option D is the correct answer. For completeness, the **--from=**, **--to=** and **--range** options do not exist for the **journalctl** command.

18. B - Topic 109.2

In Linux, **nmcli** is a command-line tool for controlling NetworkManager and reporting network status. This utility allows both users and scripts to interact with NetworkManager and is used to perform several network tasks such as managing network connections (check the man pages to see the full list of activities). This makes option B the correct answer. For completeness, **nmtui** is a curses-based TUI (Text User Interface) application that provides a text interface that allows users to interact with NetworkManager, while the **nmctl** and **nmcmd** utilities do not exist.

19.C - Topic 107.1

The **chage** command is used to change user password expiry information. In particular, the **-M** option of this command sets the maximum number of days during which a password is valid. After that period the user must change his password before being able to use his account. This makes option C the correct answer.

20.B - Topic 107.1

The **chsh** command is used to change the login shell. In order to accomplish this task, you can use this command with the **-s (--shell)** option followed by the new login shell you want to use. This command can be used by root and by ordinary users, making option B correct and option A incorrect. The command in option D has a correct syntax and assigns a new login shell to the specified user, but it can only be used by root and by users with root privileges. Finally, an ordinary user can only read the information in **/etc/passwd**, but cannot edit this file, contrary to what is indicated in option C. In general, even if you are acting as root, do not edit user and group files directly, but always use command-line tools or graphical applications provided with your distribution for this purpose.

21.D - Topic 107.3

In Linux, **LC_ALL** is an environment variable that, when set, overrides all **locale categories** (thus all the **LC_** variables such as **LC_NUMERIC**, **LC_TIME**, **LC_COLLATE**, **LC_MESSAGES** and so on). Therefore, option D is the correct answer.

22.E - Topic 108.2

The priority represents the importance of the message to be logged. Starting from the least important, the priority values and their corresponding purpose and number are: **debug** (debugging messages - 7), **info** (information messages of normal operation - 6), **notice** (abnormal messages that may be noteworthy, but that do not cause concern - 5), **warning** (warnings or messages about non imminent errors - 4), **err** (non-urgent error messages - 3), **crit** (critical error messages concerning secondary systems - 2), **alert** (critical error messages concerning primary systems that immediately require the user's attention - 1), and **emerg** (panic messages due to, for example, unstable or unusable system - 0). Therefore, option E is the correct answer.

23.C - Topic 110.2

The **/etc/xinetd.d** directory contains a configuration file for each service managed by **xinetd**, making option C the correct answer.

24.B - Topic 108.3

In Linux, **/etc/aliases** (or sometimes **/etc/mail/aliases**) is the mail alias file, in which root or users with root privileges can define one or more destinations for all the incoming e-mails of a specified username. An ordinary user cannot edit this file, but can forward all his incoming e-mails by editing the **.forward** file in his home directory or creating a new one if it doesn't exist. Therefore, the **bar** user should edit his **.forward** file in his home directory by entering only the external address to which to forward his mail, making option B the correct answer.

25.C, D - Topic 109.2

The **nmcli** command followed by the **connection** object is used to start, stop, and manage network connections. In particular, you can use the **add** subcommand to add a new connection and the **connection.type** property (or **type** alias) defines the type of connection to add. Some valid connection types are: ethernet, wifi, wimax, pppoe, gsm, bluetooth, vlan, bond, bond-slave, team, team-slave, bridge, bridge-slave, and vpn (consult the man pages of your distribution to see the full list of connection types supported by NetworkManager). Therefore, options C and D are the correct answers.

26.B, D - Topic 105.1

Shell variables are only available in the current working shell. If you want to make a shell variable visible (thus usable) in a child process (such as a shell script), you must **export** it as stated in option B. You can also accomplish the same task using the **declare** command with the **-x** option, making also option D the correct answer. For completeness, option C has a wrong syntax, while options A and E contain invalid commands.

27. B - Topic 108.4

The **lpq** command is used to show the current print queue status on the default printer or on a specific printer. In particular, it returns the rank, the owner, the job number, the file name and the file size of each print job in the queue of the specified printer. This makes option B the correct answer.

28. D - Topic 110.1

In Linux, **netstat** can be used as an auditing tool to check open ports on a system. In particular, the **-lu** option of this command shows only the listening UDP ports, making option D the correct answer. For completeness, option A shows all UDP ports (listening and non-listening), option B lists only the listening TCP ports, and option C lists the statistics for TCP ports. Finally remember that **netstat** is now obsolete and has been replaced by **ss**.

29. C - Topic 107.2

Calendar events are used by timer units to specify the date and time a job is executed. The ***:0/1** specification is equivalent to ***-*-* *:00/01:00**, which indicates that the job is executed every minute (* means any value and / allows you to specify step values). This makes option C the correct answer. Refer to answer 56 of Practice Exam 1 to see the right syntax to use with **OnCalendar** events.

30. A - Topic 108.4

The **cupsenable** command is used to start a stopped printer. In particular, you can use the **-c** option of this command to also delete all jobs queued on the specified printer. Therefore, option A is the correct answer. For completeness, the **-d**, **-C**, and **-D** options do not exist for the **cupsenable** command.

31. C - Topic 110.3

In public key authentication, the **~/.ssh/authorized_keys** file (or sometimes **~/.ssh/authorized_keys2**) on the remote OpenSSH server specifies the SSH public keys that can be used for logging into the user account for which the file is configured. This makes option C the correct answer.

32. B - Topic 105.1

Working with the bash shell, you can display the Process ID of the current shell using the **echo $$** command, the Parent Process ID using the **echo $PPID** command, the Process ID of the last job running in background using the echo **$!** command, and the exit code of the last executed command using the **echo $?** command. You can use a single **echo** command to display all these values. Therefore, option B is the correct answer. For completeness, the **PID** and **EXIT** variables do not exist by default.

33. A - Topic 109.4

In Linux, **/etc/hosts** is a simple text file that holds mappings of IP addresses to hostnames on a single computer. For each host you should have only one line with the following syntax: **IPaddress hostname [aliases]**. The fields of each entry are separated by any number of spaces and/or tabs. Therefore, option A is the correct answer.

34. C - Topic 105.2

The command specified in the question concatenates the **echo** command with a loop (**while**) through the pipe (|) operator. As a result, the output of **echo** is used as input of the loop construct: **var1** is assigned the string **This**, **var2** is assigned the string **sequence**, **var3** is assigned the string **is** and **var4** is assigned the string **put in 4 variables**. These variables are printed to the bash prompt in the following order: **var4**, **var3**, **var2** and **var1,** and therefore the string **put in 4 variables is sequence This** is displayed. This makes option C the correct answer.

35.B - Topic 107.1

The **gpasswd** command is used to administer the groups in the system and change their password. In particular, the **-a** option of this command followed by a user account is used to add that user account to a specified group, making option B the correct answer. For completeness, option C reverses the user account and group, while options A and D specify an invalid command.

36.B - Topic 109.3

The **hostname** command is used to show or set the hostname of a local machine. In particular, only a user with root privileges can change the hostname, but this effect is temporary and lasts until the next reboot (or until a new change is made). This makes option B the correct answer. For completeness, if you want to permanently set the hostname of your local machine by acting as root, you should edit a configuration file, specific for the distribution used (for example, **/etc/hostname**).

37.D - Topic 108.1

The **pool.ntp.org** subdomain is dedicated to a big virtual cluster of public NTP servers. You can configure your NTP server to use this pool of time servers as a time source and in particular you can specify either **pool.ntp.org** or a numbered host within this subdomain (for example **0.pool.ntp.org**). Furthermore, you can use time servers related to a well-defined geographical area, adding a geographical name to the subdomain name (for example **europe.pool.ntp.org**), and then also a numbered host within this new subdomain (for example **0.europe.pool.ntp.org**). Therefore, option D is the correct answer.

38.A, B, D - Topic 109.3

The **netstat** command is used to display various network information such as network connections, routing tables, interface statistics, masquerade connections, and multicast membership. Therefore, options A, B and D are the correct answers. For completeness, to add and delete routes, you can use the **route** legacy net tool or the **ip** command, while to configure a network interface, you can use the **ifconfig** legacy net tool or the **ip** command. Also note that **netstat** is obsolete and its replacement is **ss**.

39. D - Topic 110.3

In Linux, to connect to a remote machine, you can use the **ssh remote-machine** command, where **remote-machine** can be an IP address or a machine name (in this case the current user is used when accessing the remote server). You can specify a different port number through the **-p** (or **-o Port=**) option. Therefore, the right command to use is **ssh -o Port=2112 192.168.1.10** (or alternatively **ssh -p 2112 192.168.1.10**), making option D the correct answer.

40. A, C - Topic 106.1

The **xorg.conf** file consists of a series of sections that can be present in any order. In particular, the **Monitor** section is used to set monitor options and the **InputDevice** section is used to set options related to input devices (keyboard and mouse). This makes options A and C the correct answers. Refer to the man pages for the complete list of sections.

41. A, B - Topic 106.2

In Linux, the most common display managers (also known as login managers or XDMCP servers) are: X Display Manager (XDM), KDE Display Manager (KDM), GNOME Display Manager (GDM)/GNOME Display Manager 3 (GDM3), LXDE Display Manager (LXDM), and Light Display Manager (LightDM). Therefore, options A and B are the correct answers. Refer to answer 46 of Practice Exam 1 for a detailed explanation of the role of a display manager.

42. C - Topic 106.1

The question assumes that you want to sit on the machine with IP address 192.168.1.100 (local machine) and run a graphical application located on the machine with IP address 192.168.5.10 (remote machine). The question also assumes that the machine with IP address 192.168.5.10 is allowed to connect to the machine with IP address 192.168.1.100. Therefore, to achieve the goal, once connected via SSH from the local to the remote machine, you only need to type **export DISPLAY 192.168.1.100:0** in the bash shell. In fact, this command tells the remote machine to use the machine where you sit for the display of the graphical applications that you run remotely. In particular, it sets the **DISPLAY** environment variable, indicating where the X server can be found (the machine with IP 192.168.1.100) and which display of the X server should be used (display number 0). This makes option C the correct answer.

43. A - Topic 109.1

An IPv6 address consists of 128 bits (eight groups of four hexadecimal digits separated by colons, thus 16 bits for each group). This makes option A the correct answer.

44. /etc/resolv.conf - Topic 109.4

In Linux, **/etc/resolv.conf** is the resolver configuration file that holds the main information on name resolution. In this file you can use the **nameserver** keyword to specify the IP address of the server used for name resolution (you can include up to three **nameserver** lines), and the **search** keyword to set the list of domains to search when resolving a name (usually only the local domain name is specified). For completeness, remember that instead of **search** you can also find the **domain** directive, which is used to set the local domain name of your machine (in particular, **domain** and **search** are mutually exclusive and if both are specified, the last will take the precedence over the other).

45. B, D - Topic 110.1

The **lsof** and **fuser** commands are generally used to audit network ports. These two commands are also useful for identifying which processes are accessing a filesystem, especially when a device busy error occurs during the device unmount operation. Once these processes are identified, you can kill them, and then unmount the filesystem. This makes options B and D the correct answers. For completeness, the **lsop**, **listproc**, and **fpo** commands are invalid.

46. C - Topic 107.1

The **passwd** command can be used to change the password of a user account. In particular, an ordinary user can change his password and the root user can change the password of any user. Therefore, a system administrator can change the password of the **foo** user simply by typing **passwd foo**. This makes option C the correct answer. For completeness, the **passwd** command with the **-u** option is used to unlock a user account, while the **chpass** command do not exist.

47. D - Topic 108.3

The mail alias file is typically **/etc/aliases**, but in some distributions you may find **/etc/mail/aliases** instead of **/etc/aliases**. Therefore, option D is the correct answer.

48. /etc/nsswitch.conf - Topic 109.2

In Linux, **/etc/nsswitch.conf** is the name service switch configuration file, which can be used to specify the order in which hostnames are resolved. Actually this file supports many more options, so check the man pages for details.

49. C - Topic 109.1

The TCP and UDP ports 0 to 1023 are the so-called known-ports. In particular, the HTTP service is assigned to TCP port 80, the HTTPS service is assigned to TCP port 443, the SMTP service is assigned to TCP port 25, the IMAP service is assigned to TCP port 143, the FTP service is assigned to TCP port 21, the SSH service is assigned to TCP port 22, the Telnet service is assigned to TCP port 23, and the POP3 service is assigned to TCP port 110. Therefore, option C is the correct answer.

50. A, D - Topic 107.2

The **at** utility is used to schedule one or more commands to be executed at a specific time in the future. In particular, the **-r** option of this command is used to delete jobs identified by their job number from the **at** queue. Typing **at -r** is equivalent to executing the **atrm** command. Therefore, options A and D are the correct answers. For completeness, the **at** command does not have the **--remove** and **--delete** options, while the **atdel** command does not exist.

51. C - Topic 109.3

For IPv6 addresses, the equivalent commands for **ping** and **traceroute** are **ping6** and **traceroute6**. Therefore, option C is the correct answer.

52. A - Topic 105.2

The term **shebang** refers to a sequence of characters starting with **#!** which is inserted at the beginning of a script to identify the shell used to run it. For example, the **shebang** line for a bash script is **#!/bin/bash**. This makes option A the correct answer.

53. A - Topic 108.2

The **logger** command provides a shell command interface to the **syslog** system log module and is therefore used to add messages to the system log from the command line or from other files. It is very useful in scripts to log important information, such as the start and end date of a particular task as and comments for debugging purposes. This makes option A the correct answer.

54. A - Topic 110.1

In Linux, **ulimit** is a bash built-in command used to set the shell resource usage limits and its options define what should be limited (for example, the size of core dumps, the number of processes that a user can run, the maximum size of files created by the shell, and so on). Therefore, option A is the correct answer.

55. B - Topic 106.3

Linux distributions include accessibility tools that can help people with disabilities. For example, a screen reader is a text-to-speech system for blind or visually impaired users that translates on-screen information into speech. Furthermore, some screen readers, such as **Orca**, can also provide information in braille. This makes option B the correct answer.

56. A - Topic 110.2

If your Linux system uses shadow passwords, **/etc/passwd** and **/etc/group** contain an **x** in the second field of each line instead of the encrypted passwords for users and groups because the encrypted passwords are stored in **/etc/shadow** and **/etc/gshadow**. As a result, your system has better security because ordinary users cannot see password hashes (remember that **/etc/passwd** and **/etc/group** are world-readable, but **/etc/shadow** and **/etc/gshadow** are readable only by root and users with root privileges). This makes option A correct and options B and C incorrect. Options D and E contain only good rules to follow when choosing a password and are therefore incorrect.

57. B - Topic 109.1

In Linux, the **/etc/services** file provides a mapping between Internet network services and their assigned port numbers and protocol types. Each line describes one service and has the following syntax: **service-name port/protocol [aliases]**. Therefore, option B is the correct answer.

58. B - Topic 110.3

In Linux, **gpg** is a useful tool that provides digital encryption and signing services using the OpenPGP standard. In particular, the **--sign** (or **-s**) option is used to make a signature, while the **--clearsign** option is used to make a clear text signature. The **--sign** option creates a **.gpg** file that is encrypted using the private key of the user and can only be decrypted by those who know the public key of the user who made the signature. The **--clearsign** option creates a **.asc** file, adding only an encrypted signature (created using the private key of the user) that can be verified by those who know the public key of the user who made the clear text signature (the message text remains unencrypted). This makes option B the correct answer. For completeness, the **--plaintext, --psign**, and **--cleartext** options do not exist for the **gpg** command.

59.A - Topic 109.3

The **ip** command is used to show and manipulate routing, devices, policy routing and tunnels. In particular, you can use the **ip route add** command to add a new route, and the **ip route add default via** command followed by an IP address to set the machine with that IP address as the default gateway for your system (in general, the **route** object identifies a routing table entry). This makes option A the correct answer. For completeness, the **ip link set** command changes the device attributes and the **link** object identifies a network device.

60.D - Topic 107.1

The **useradd** command is used to create a new user or update default new user information. In particular, you can use the **-u** option to create a new user account with a specific User ID (UID), the **-g** option to create a new user account with a specific Group ID (GID), the **-G** option to create a new user account by adding it to multiple secondary groups, the **-s** option to create a new user account with a specific login shell, the **-k** option to create a new user account by specifying a custom skeleton directory that contains files and directories to copy to the user's home directory, the **-h** option to display an help message, and the **-d** option to create a new user account with a custom home directory. Therefore, option D is the correct answer.

Answers to the Practice Exam 3

1. **D - Topic 105.2**

   The bash script tests the number of parameters passed to the script: if the number of parameters (**$#**) is lower than 1 (**-lt 1**), it assigns value **1** to the **VAR** variable, otherwise it assigns **2** to **VAR**. Finally, it prints the value of **VAR** to the bash prompt. Therefore, option D is the correct answer.

2. **D - Topic 107.1**

   In Linux, the **groupadd** command is used to create a new group using the values specified on the command line plus the default values from the system. This makes option D the correct answer. For completeness, the **groupmod** command is used to modify the definition of the specified group on the system and does not have the **--add** option, the **newgrp** command is used to change the current group ID during a login session, and the **newgroup** command does not exist.

3. **D - Topic 105.2**

   In Linux, command substitution is used to allow the output of a command to replace the command itself. It occurs when a command is enclosed as follows: **"$(command)"** or `` `command` ``. Then you can use command substitution to replace the **pwd** command with the name of the current working directory and assign this value to the **current_path** variable. This makes option D the correct answer. For completeness, option A assigns the **${pwd}** string to **current_path**, option B assigns the **$(pwd)** string to **current path**, and option C assigns the value of the **pwd** variable to **current_path.** Finally, remember the difference between double quotes and single quotes when working with the bash shell:

double quotes evaluate the variables between them displaying their value and allow command substitution, while single quotes do not expand variables and do not allow command substitution (they protect everything that is enclosed between them).

4. B - Topic 109.2

In Linux, **nmtui** is a curses-based TUI (Text User Interface) application for interacting with NetworkManager. This tool provides a text interface that guides the user to perform various tasks such as adding, modifying, viewing and deleting connections, activating and deactivating connections, and setting the system host name. Therefore, option B is the correct answer. For completeness, **nmcli** is a command-line tool to control NetworkManager and report network status, while **nmconfig**, **tuiconfig** and **cliconfig** do not exist.

5. D - Topic 105.1

The **PATH** environment variable contains a list of directory names separated by colons in which the shell looks for commands or programs you run at the command line. So, if you want to add a new directory to this list, you must modify the value of the **PATH** environment variable. The right syntax to use is the one shown in option D which adds two new entries (**/usr/games** and **/opt/custom**) to the list of directory names in your path (**$PATH**). Each value must be separated by colons. For completeness, remember that if you want to make the change permanent, you need to add the line to your shell startup files.

6. C - Topic 105.2

The **-d, -f, -L,** and **-e** unary operators can be used with the **test** command to perform a simple test on a specific filesystem object. In particular, **test -d** returns true if the specified filesystem object exists and is a directory, **test -f** returns true if the specified filesystem object exists and is a regular file, **test -L** returns true if the specified filesystem object exists and is a symbolic link, and **test -e** returns true if the specified filesystem object exists. Therefore, option C is the correct answer. Refer to answer 10 of the Assessment Test for a detailed description of the **test** command, and to answer 1 of the Practice Exam 1 for more information about positional parameters.

7. B - Topic 109.2

In Linux, **/etc/resolv.conf** is the resolver configuration file that holds the main information on name resolution. In this file, for example, you can set the IP address of the servers used for name resolution, and the computer's default search domain. Therefore, option B is the correct answer.

8. A - Topic 107.1

The **userdel** command is used to delete a user account and the **-r (--remove)** option of this command is used to also remove the files in the user's home directory along with the home directory itself and the user's mail spool. This makes option A the correct answer. For completeness, option B removes the **foo** directory (located in the current working directory) and its contents recursively, while options C and D contain invalid commands.

9. B - Topic 107.3

The Time Zone Database (often called **tz**) provides information on world time zones. According to this database, **Europe/Madrid** is a valid time zone specification, making option B the correct answer.

10.A - Topic 109.2

The question shows the output of the **route -n** command, which is used to display the kernel routing table on a Linux system (the **-n** option shows numerical addresses instead of trying to determine symbolic hostnames). An outgoing packet to a host in the local network 192.168.1.0 is transmitted directly to the destination over the network interface eth0, while an outgoing packet to a host in the local network 192.168.5.0 is transmitted directly to the destination over the network interface eth1. Furthermore, an outgoing packet to a host in the network 192.168.10.0 (for example to the host 192.168.10.100) is transmitted to the router 192.168.1.100 over the network interface eth0. Finally, an outgoing packet is transmitted to the default gateway (192.168.1.254) when no other route specification matches the destination IP address of the packet (default route). Therefore, option A is the correct answer.

11.D - Topic 107.1

Based on the explanation of question 32 of Practice Exam 1, option D contains a valid entry of **/etc/passwd** and is therefore the correct answer.

12.B - Topic 107.2

The entry in the question refers to a **user crontab file** and specifies the time to run the **foobar** job. In particular, the asterisk operator (*) means any value and the slash operator (/) allows you to specify step values. Therefore, **foobar** runs every fifteen minutes (***/15 * * * ***), making option B the correct answer. Refer to answer 10 of Practice Exam 1 for a detailed description of all fields in a **user crontab file**.

13.C - Topic 108.4

In Linux, the **lpr** command is used to print files and the -# option of this command sets the number of copies to print. Therefore, option C is the correct answer. For completeness, the -**m** option is used to send an email on job completion, while the -**$**, -**!**, and -**k** options do not exist.

14. B, E - Topic 108.3

The general form of a mail alias is **name: alias1, alias2, ... aliasN** where **name** is a local username to alias and **alias1, alias2, ... aliasN** are the aliases to **name**. Specifically, an alias can be a local username on the system or a username on another system (in the form **username@machine-name**) or an external e-mail address to which the e-mails are forwarded, a local file name in which e-mails are stored, another alias, a command through which e-mails are piped, and an **include** file that specifies one or more aliases. Therefore, options B and E are the correct answers. In particular, **bar: foobar, barfoo** sends the e-mails of **bar** to the **foobar** and **barfoo** users, while **foo: /home/foo/mail-folder** sends the e-mails of **foo** to the **mail-folder** file in his home directory.

15.A, B - Topic 109.1

Based on the explanation of question 4 of Practice Exam 2, the addresses reserved for private networks are: 10.10.10.10 and 172.31.22.22. Therefore, options A and B are the correct answers.

16.192.168.7.0 - Topic 109.1

The network mask is used to find out which part of an IP address is the network address and which is the host address. In particular, if the network mask is expressed in binary form, the set of binary values 1 represents the network address, while the set of binary values 0 represents the host address. The network mask 255.255.255.0 can be expressed in binary form as 11111111.11111111.11111111.00000000 and therefore for host 192.168.7.100 (11000000.10101000.00000111.01100100) the network address is 192.168.7.0 (11000000.10101000.00000111.00000000).

17.B - Topic 109.4

In Linux, **dig** is a DNS lookup utility, which can be useful for troubleshooting DNS problems. By default, it uses DNS servers in **/etc/resolv.conf**, but a different DNS server can be specified on the command line using **@serverDNS**. Therefore, if you are not sure of the result of the query performed by the DNS servers in **/etc/resolv.conf**, you can run another query by specifying an alternative DNS server (such as Google's). This makes option B the correct answer. For completeness, note that the **dig** utility does not have the **-s**, **-o** and **--debug** options.

18.B - Topic 105.1

Acting as root, you define an alias named **foovalue** that echoes a string with the value of the **foo** variable. If you use double quotation marks in your alias, the shell evaluates any variable references at the time the alias is defined, while if you use single quotation marks, the shell evaluates any variable references at the time the alias is executed. This makes option B the correct answer.

19. A - Topic 105.1

When you type the **su - foobar** command, the user is switched and a login shell is invoked. So, after entering the password for **foobar**, the new bash login shell runs several profile scripts: first it runs **/etc/profile** (if it exists) along with any **.sh** files in **/etc/profile.d**, and then checks the **/home/foobar/.bash_profile**, **/home/foobar/.bash_login**, and **/home/foobar/.profile** files, in that order, and runs the first one that it finds. This makes option A the correct answer.

20. A - Topic 106.1

The question assumes that you want to sit on the machine with IP address 192.168.1.100 (local machine) and run a graphical application located on the machine with IP address 192.168.5.10 (remote machine). The question also assumes that you have correctly exported the **DISPLAY** variable. So, the last thing to do is to add the machine with IP address 192.168.5.10 to the list of machines from which the X server on the machine with IP address 192.168.1.100 accepts connections. You can do this using the **xhost 192.168.5.10** command on the machine with IP address 192.168.1.100. Therefore, option A is the correct answer. Refer to answer 2 of Practice Exam 1 for a detailed description of the **xhost** command.

21. C, D - Topic109.3

In Linux, **netcat** (or **nc** as the actual program is named) is a simple utility which reads and writes data across network connections using TCP or UDP protocol. In the simplest usage (**nc host port**), it creates a TCP connection to the specified port on the target host, sending the standard input to the host, and anything that comes back across the connection is sent to the standard output until the connection shuts down. In addition to this simple feature of network debugging tool, **netcat** can also be used to perform many other useful tasks (see the man pages for details), and can be used directly or driven by other programs or scripts. Therefore, options C and D are the correct answers.

22. /etc/shadow - Topic 107.1

In Linux, **/etc/shadow** is a file of nine colon-delimited fields that contains encrypted passwords of the users in the system, each on a separate line. Refer to answer 14 of Practice Exam 1 for the complete description of each field in this file.

23. D - Topic 110.3

In Linux, **ssh-agent** is an authentication agent that holds private keys for public key authentication and their passphrase, and allows to permanently authenticate a terminal session so that a passphrase can be typed only once at the beginning of the session and not every time you log in to a remote machine using ssh. To test it, you can start a bash session via **ssh-agent** and in this new shell session add the private key to the authentication agent. You can see that the passphrase is asked only at this point and every time you log in to a remote system (that has your public key) within this same session, you don't need to rewrite it. If it is useful, you can insert **ssh-agent** in your usual login procedure. Therefore, option D is the correct answer.

24. C - Topic 110.1

The **/etc/security/limits.conf** file is used to limit users' access to system resources. For example, by editing this file, you can limit the size of core files, the size of files created by a user, the maximum number of logins for a user (except the one with UID 0), the maximum number of all logins on the system, and so on. Therefore, option C is the correct answer.

25. B - Topic 105.2

In bash, if you want to assign the value of a variable named **VAR1** to a variable named **VAR2**, you must use **VAR2=$VAR1**, by prefixing the symbol **$** to **VAR1** (**$** is used to access the value stored in the **VAR1** variable). Therefore, option B is the correct answer. For completeness, option A assigns the string **VAR1** to the **VAR2** variable, option C assigns the result of the **VAR1** command to the **VAR2** variable, and option D redirects the output of the **VAR1** command to the **VAR2** file.

26.C - Topic 107.3

The **locale** command is used to get **locale-specific information**. In particular, you can use the **--all-locales** (or **-a**) option to display the list of all available **locales** on your system, making option C the correct answer.

27.C - Topic 109.1

In TCP/IP networks, 127.0.0.1 is the localhost IPv4 address that identifies the machine you are using. The equivalent IPv6 address is ::1, making option C the correct answer.

28.B - Topic 106.1

The X Window System, commonly referred to as X, is a system for managing GUIs (Graphical User Interface) on single machines and within distributed networks. X.org-X11 is one implementation of X that has grown in popularity in the last years. Its main configuration file is **xorg.conf**, which is composed of a series of sections, each of which controls a particular aspect of X, such as input devices (mouse and keyboard), monitor, video card, and so on. These sections can be present in any order and begin with the keyword **Section** and end with **EndSection**. This makes option B the correct answer.

29.A, B - Topic 110.1

If you want to show who is currently logged into the system, you can use the **who** and **w** commands. In particular, the first simply prints information about users who are currently logged in, while the second shows who is logged in, what they are doing, and statistics on CPU usage. Therefore, options A and B are the correct answers. For completeness, the **wc** command prints newline, word, and byte counts for each specified file, while the **wis** and **wislogged** commands do not exist.

30. D - Topic 109.3

The **tracepath** command (or **tracepath6** for IPv6) is used to trace path to a destination discovering MTU (Maximum Transmission Unit) along this path. It is similar to **traceroute** (or **traceroute6**), but does not require root privileges. Therefore, option D is the correct answer.

31. A - Topic 110.2

In Linux, **/etc/xinetd.conf** is the Extended Internet Services Daemon configuration file that determines the services provided by **xinetd**. If your system uses several configuration files instead of an integrated configuration file, you can put the global default options that affect each service under the **xinetd** control in **/etc/xinetd.conf** and you can put the configuration files for each specific service managed by **xinetd** in the **/etc/xinetd.d** directory. This makes option A the correct answer.

32. B - Topic 109.1

As described in answer 49 of Practice Exam 2, TCP and UDP ports 0 to 1023 are the so-called known-ports. In particular, the Telnet service is assigned to TCP port 23, while the NTP service is assigned to UDP port 123. Therefore, option B is the correct answer.

33. A, E - Topic 109.3

The **ip** command is used to show and manipulate routing, devices, policy routing and tunnels. The set of possible actions depends on the object type specified after **ip**. For example, you can display a list of all network interfaces, configure a network interface, bring interfaces up or down, and display and alter the kernel routing table (check the man pages to see the complete list of activities you can do). This makes options A and E the correct answers. For completeness, to permanently change the order in which name resolution is performed, you can edit the **/etc/nsswitch.conf** configuration file, to change the hostname of the system on the fly, you can use the **hostname** command, and to perform DNS lookups, you can use the **nslookup**, **host**, and **dig** commands.

34.A - Topic 109.3

As described in the previous question, **ip** is used to show and manipulate routing, devices, policy routing and tunnels. In particular, the **ip route add** command is used to add a new route and option A contains the right syntax to use (**-net**, **-gw**, and **-via** in options B and C are invalid). For completeness, the **route** command is a legacy net tool that can be used to add routes, but the syntax in options D and E is incorrect (you do not need to put the - character in front of **netmask, gw**, and **dev**, and also **-via** is not recognized by **route**).

35.A- Topic 107.3

The **TZ** environment variable is used to set a specific time zone. This variable is usually used if the time zone you want to set is different from that of your computer. This makes option A the correct answer. For completeness, the **LANG** environment variable is normally used to specify a **locale**, while **/etc/localtime** cannot be edited manually (it is the local time zone configuration file, but it is not plain-text).

36.B - Topic 108.3

An ordinary user can forward all his incoming e-mails by editing the **.forward** file in his home directory or creating a new one if it doesn't exist. So, if the user named **barfoo** wants to forward his mail to other users, he can specify multiple entries in this file separated by a comma or a new line. Furthermore, he can add the **\barfoo** entry to also deliver the mail directly to his local mailbox (the \ character before **barfoo** avoids further alias expansions). Therefore, option B is the correct answer.

37.C - Topic 106.3

A screen reader is a text-to-speech system for blind or visually impaired users that translates on-screen information into speech (or Braille). The Mouse Keys accessibility feature enables users to use the keyboard's numeric keypad as a pointing device to emulate the mouse. The on-screen keyboard displays a visual keyboard on the screen and allows you to select keys using the mouse or another pointing device. A screen magnifier tool enlarges part of the screen when the mouse cursor passes over a section of the viewing area so that people with visual impairments can better see words and images. Therefore, option C is the correct answer.

38.C - Topic 108.3

Since **sendmail** has been the standard MTA on Unix-like systems for years, other MTAs have implemented **sendmail emulation layer commands** to maintain compatibility with it. Therefore, many MTAs provide the **sendmail** command for compatibility reasons, making option C the correct answer. For completeness, **sendmail -bp** is often implemented as a **sendmail emulation layer command** to display the mail queue, while the **postq** command does not exist.

39.C - Topic 105.1

The **declare** command is a bash built-in that is used to declare shell variables and functions, set their attributes, and display their values. A read-only variable can be declared using the **declare -r** command and cannot be unset. In addition, new values cannot be assigned to this variable by subsequent assignment statements. Therefore, if you need to assign a value to a read-only variable, you can do so during its declaration, making option C the correct answer. For completeness, the **declare** command does not have the **--read-only** and **-R** options.

40.A - Topic 108.2

In Linux, the **journalctl** command is used to query the contents of the systemd journal and the **-b** option of this command is used to show messages from a specific boot. For example, assuming that you are looking at the logs of your machine and that the last boot is the current one, you can use **-b -0** or simply **-b** to show messages from the last boot, and **-b -1** to show messages from the previous one (the boot before last). This makes option A the correct answer. For completeness, the **-n** option is used to show the most recent journal events and limit the number of events shown, while the **--boot-select** and **--boot-number** options do not exist.

41. nameserver - Topic 109.4

As described in answer 44 of Practice Exam 2, the **nameserver** keyword in the **/etc/resolv.conf** configuration file specifies the IP address of a server used for name resolution. For completeness, remember that you can include up to three **nameserver** lines.

42. C - Topic 110.3

In Linux, **gpg** is a useful tool that provides digital encryption and signing services using the OpenPGP standard. In particular, if you have a signed **.gpg** file, you can use the **--verify** option of **gpg** to verify its signature, making option C the correct answer. For completeness, remember that if you want to read the file, you must decrypt it using the **--decrypt** option (in any case you must have the correct key in your keyring).

43. D - Topic 110.2

The **only_from** attribute is used within a specific service configuration file managed by **xinetd** to specify the remote hosts to which the particular service is available (refer to the man pages to see the possible ways in which you can specify the remote hosts). Therefore, option D is the correct answer. For completeness, the **access_from**, **allow**, and **restrict** attributes do not exist.

44. B - Topic 110.3

~/.ssh/id_rsa and **~/.ssh/id_rsa.pub**, **~/.ssh/id_dsa** and **~/.ssh/id_dsa.pub**, **~/.ssh/id_ecdsa** and **~/.ssh/id_ecdsa.pub**, and **~/.ssh/id_ed25519** and **~/.ssh/id_ed25519.pub** are typical pairs of private and public user keys, which are created based on the type of key specified using the **-t** option of the **ssh-keygen** command. Instead, **/etc/ssh/ssh_host_rsa_key** and **/etc/ssh/ssh_host_rsa_key.pub**, **/etc/ssh/ssh_host_dsa_key** and **/etc/ssh/ssh_host_dsa_key.pub**, **/etc/ssh/ssh_host_ecdsa_key** and **/etc/ssh/ssh_host_ecdsa_key.pub**, and **/etc/ssh/ssh_host_ed25519_key** and **/etc/ssh/ssh_host_ed25519_key.pub** are private and public host authentication keys, which are automatically generated when an OpenSSH server is installed, but can also be regenerated at any time (remember that each host can have public and private host keys for each algorithm). This makes option B the correct answer.

45. Storage - Topic 108.2

In **journald.conf**, the **Storage** option controls where to store journal data. The list of possible values for this option is: **none** to turn off the storage of all journal log data, **volatile** to store journal log data only in memory below the **/run/log/journal** hierarchy (which is created if needed), **persistent** to store journal log data preferably on disk below the **/var/log/journal** hierarchy (which is created if needed), with a fallback to **/run/log/journal** (which is created if needed) during early boot and if the disk is not writable, and **auto** which is similar to **persistent**, but the directory **/var/log/journal** is not created if needed.

46. A - Topic 110.2

When shadow passwords are used, encrypted passwords for users and groups are stored in **/etc/shadow** and **/etc/gshadow**. As a result, you can see an **x** in the second field of **/etc/passwd** and **/etc/group** instead of encrypted user and group passwords. Therefore, option A is the correct answer. As explained in answer 56 of Practice Exam 2, a system that uses shadow passwords has better security because ordinary users cannot see password hashes (remember that **/etc/shadow** and **/etc/gshadow** are readable only by root and by users with root privileges, while **/etc/passwd** and **/etc/group** are world-readable).

47. A - Topic 107.2

The **at** utility is used to schedule one or more commands to be executed at a specific time in the future. In particular, **at -l** (or also **atq**) is used to list the user's pending **at jobs**, unless the user is root or a user with root privileges. In this case, the **at jobs** of all users are listed. This makes option A the correct answer. For completeness, the **at -r** command (or also **atrm**) is used to delete **at jobs**, the **at -f** command is used to read the **at job** from the specified file rather than standard input, and the **at -v** command is used to show the time the **at job** will be executed before reading the job.

48.C - Topic 110.3

A keyring is a file that holds GPG keys. In particular, in version 1.4 of GnuPG, **~/.gnupg/secring.gpg** is the secret keyring, while **~/.gnupg/pubring.gpg** is the public keyring. Therefore, option C is the correct answer. For completeness, remember that the new version of GnuPG has new features that bring significant changes even in the management of the private and public keyring.

49.B - Topic 108.1

The **ntpdate** command is used to set the system time from an NTP server, making option B the correct answer. This command is deprecated and in the new Linux distributions you can use **ntpd -q** to perform the same task.

50.B - Topic 107.2

In Linux, **/etc/crontab** is a system-wide **crontab file**, which can be edited only by root and by users with root privileges. Each line in this file contains seven fields separated by a space: the **minute of the hour** (0 - 59), the **hour of the day** (0 - 23), the **day of the month** (1 - 31), the **month of the year** (1 - 12), the **day of the week** (0 - 7 with Sunday=0 or 7), the **account name to be used when executing the job**, and the **command to run**. Therefore, option B is the correct answer.

51.D - Topic 108.2

In **/etc/rsyslog.conf**, you can filter log messages through the combination of **facility** and **priority**, often referred to as a **selector**, using the **facility.priority** syntax. An asterisk (*) is used to define all **facilities** or all **priorities**. Therefore, *.* means all log messages (all **facilities** and all **priorities**), making option D the correct answer. Remember that a **facility** is the subsystem that generates a specific log message, and a **priority** is the importance of the message to be logged.

52.C - Topic 109.2

In Linux, **nmcli** is a command-line tool for controlling NetworkManager and reporting network status. In particular, you can use the **nmcli device wifi list** command (the **list** subcommand can also be omitted) to list available Wi-Fi access points known to NetworkManager (the **device** object is used to show and manage network interfaces). This makes option C the correct answer. For completeness, the **con** (**connection**) object is used to start, stop, and manage network connections but it does not have the **wifi** subcommand, while the **wifi** and **interface** objects do not exist.

53.B, D - Topic 106.2

A desktop environment is a suite of tools, graphical themes, programs and libraries (for example window managers, file managers, display managers, browsers, text editors, widgets, and so on) for managing the desktop. In Linux, some of the most important desktop environments are: GNOME, KDE/KDE Plasma, Xfce, MATE, Cinnamon, and LXDE. Therefore, options B and D are the correct answers. For completeness, Exim is a Mail Transfer Agent (MTA), while GDM and KDM are two common display managers (note that a display manager is only a component of a desktop environment).

54.A - Topic 110.1

As described in answer 28 of Practice Exam 2, the **netstat** command can be used to check open ports on a Linux system. In particular, the **-a** or **--all** option of this command is used to list all ports (both listening and non-listening sockets), making option A the correct answer. Remember, however, that **netstat** is now obsolete and has been replaced by **ss**.

55.C - Topic 108.1

In Linux, **chrony** and **ntpd** are two different implementations of the Network Time Protocol. In particular, **chrony** is designed for systems that are frequently suspended, powered off or disconnected from the network, while **ntpd** is designed for systems that are permanently turned on and connected to the network. The main configuration file is **/etc/chrony.conf** for **chrony** and **/etc/ntp.conf** for **ntpd**. Both of these files have many directives such as **server**, which is used to specify an NTP server that can act as a time source. This makes option C the correct answer.

56. D - Topic 107.1

In Linux, **/etc/passwd** is a world-readable file: all users can read it, but only root and users with root privileges can edit it. When shadow passwords are used, you can see an **x** in the second field of **/etc/passwd**, which is therefore shadowed for security reasons. As a result, the password hashes of the user accounts are stored in **/etc/shadow**, which is a file readable only by root and by users with root privileges. Other users are not allowed to read this file directly so that they cannot gather the password hashes of the user accounts defined in the system. This makes option D the correct answer.

57. A - Topic 107.2

Using systemd, you can schedule one-time jobs with the **systemd-run** command. In fact, **systemd-run** is used to create and start a transient **.service** or **.scope** unit, and run the specified command in it. Furthermore, **systemd-run** can also be used to create and start a transient **.path**, **.socket**, or **.timer** unit, which activates a **.service** unit when elapsing. Therefore, if you want to run a pre-existing **foobar.service** file that does not have a timer file after a certain time has elapsed, you can use the **systemd-run** command, defining a monotonic timer with the **--on-active** option and specifying the service with **--unit**. This makes option A the correct answer.

58. D - Topic 108.4

The **lprm** command is used to cancel jobs that have been queued for printing. In particular, you can specify one or more IDs to cancel the corresponding print jobs, and use the - option to cancel all jobs. If no arguments are supplied, the current job on the default printer is canceled. As for the **lpr** and **lpq** commands, a particular printer can be specified through the -P option, otherwise the default printer is used. Therefore, option D is the correct answer.

59. A - Topic 108.2

The **logrotate** command is used to manage log files and is usually run as a **cron job**. In particular, **logrotate** allows automatic rotation, compression, removal and mailing of system logs. Therefore, option A is the correct answer. Remember that the log rotation configuration for all log files is specified in **/etc/logrotate.conf**, which also contains general settings and usually refers to a set of files in the **/etc/logrotate.d** directory for managing specific logs.

60. D - Topic 108.1

In Linux, **chronyc** is a command-line interface program that is used to monitor the performance of **chronyd** and to change various operating parameters whilst it is running. In particular, the **sources** subcommand is used to display information about the current time sources that **chronyd** is accessing, making option D the correct answer. For completeness, the **timesourcectl** and **chronyctl** commands do not exist.

Answers to the Practice Exam 4

1. **A, B - Topic 105.2**

   A **for** construct is a loop that executes a series of commands zero or more times. The simplest **for statement** that can be used to print the numbers between 0 and 9 is: **for i in 0 1 2 3 4 5 6 7 8 9;do echo $i;done**. You can replace the list of numbers with the syntax **{0..9}** which tells bash to iterate for each value between 0 and 9. This makes option A the correct answer. Note that the commands that are executed in each cycle are surrounded by the words **do** and **done**, and that **i** is the variable that takes different values during each cycle (remember to insert semicolon to separate the list of commands in each cycle and always before **do** and **done**). You can also use a C-like syntax to accomplish the same task as stated in option B. The other options give a syntax error and are therefore incorrect.

2. **B - Topic 106.1**

   The **xinit** program is used to manually start the X Window System server and a first client program on systems that cannot start X automatically or in environments that use multiple window systems. The **startx** command is a front end to **xinit** that provides a somewhat nicer user interface for running a single session of the X Window System. In particular, **xinit** and **startx** take an optional client program argument, but are often executed without arguments. In such cases, to determine the client to run, they first look for a file called **.xinitrc** in the user's home directory and, if it is not found, they use the **xinitrc** file in the **xinit** library directory. This script is useful to run client programs depending on X and eventually set environment variables on X server startup. This makes option B the correct answer.

3. A - Topic 107.3

Option A contains the exact procedure to change the time zone on a Linux system: first you need to delete the current **/etc/localtime** file and then you need to replace it with a symbolic link or a copy of the new time zone file chosen within the **/usr/share/zoneinfo** directory. Remember to check if your distribution also provides text-mode or GUI tools that can help you accomplish the same task. For completeness, **/etc/localtime** is the local time zone configuration file, but is not plain-text and cannot be edited manually, the **/etc/tzdata** file does not exist by default, and the **updatetz** command is invalid.

4. C - Topic 108.3

In Linux, the **mail** command is used to send and receive mail among users. In particular, you can use input redirection to send the contents of a file as the body of the e-mail, and the **-s** option to specify the e-mail subject. Therefore, option C is the correct answer. For completeness, the **-b** option is used to send blind carbon copies, while the **-r** option does not exist.

5. B - Topic 110.2

As described in answer 38 of Practice Exam 1, the **/etc/nologin** file prevents all ordinary users from logging into the system. In particular, if this file exists and is readable, only root can log in to the system, and ordinary users are shown the contents of this file and their logins are refused. Therefore, option B is the correct answer.

6. B - Topic 107.2

When editing the **crontab** file, you can use special strings that define the time to run the specified scheduled job. For example, you can use **@reboot** to run it once at startup, **@yearly** (or **@annually**) to run it once a year (the same of **0 0 1 1 ***), **@monthly** to run it once a month (the same of **0 0 1 * ***), **@weekly** to run it once a week (the same of **0 0 * * 0**), **@daily** (or **@midnight**) to run it once a day (the same of **0 0 * * ***), and **@hourly** to run it once an hour (the same of **0 * * * ***). Therefore, option B is the correct answer.

7. A - Topic 108.4

The **cupsenable** and **cupsdisable** commands are used to start and stop a specific printer respectively. Therefore, option A is the correct answer.

8. C - Topic 108.3

Option C describes exactly the meaning of the entry specified in the **/etc/aliases** file. In fact, all e-mails addressed to **root** on the system are forwarded to the local user named **foo**. Refer to answer 14 of Practice Exam 3 to see the general syntax of a mail alias.

9. C - Topic 105.1

The **env** command is used to print a list of the current environment variables or to run another program in a custom environment without modifying the current one. In particular, the **-u** option of this command removes the specified variables from the new environment, while the **-i** option starts an empty environment. Therefore, **env** executes the **bash -c 'echo $VAR $VAR1'** command, removing the **VAR** variable (**-u VAR**) from the new environment. As a result, the bash shell only prints the value of **VAR1**, making option C the correct answer.

10. B - Topic 109.1

The network mask 255.255.255.192 can be expressed in binary form as 11111111.11111111.11111111.11000000. As you can see, the first 26 bits are set to 1 and therefore the network mask corresponds to /26 in the CIDR notation, making option B the correct answer.

11. sudo - Topic 110.1

The **sudo** command allows a permitted user to execute a command as the superuser or another user, according to the specifications in the **/etc/sudoers** file. Therefore, the **foobar** user can use **sudo** to run a command with root privileges. Remember that **sudo** requires that users authenticate themselves with a password (by default the user's password), and that once authenticated, users can use **sudo** without a password for five minutes unless configured differently in **/etc/sudoers** (this time can be extended by another five minutes or by what is set in **/etc/sudoers** using the **sudo -v** command).

12.C - Topic 107.2

Based on the explanation of question 10 of Practice Exam 1, the value 12 represents the **minutes** field, making option C the correct answer.

13.D - Topic 106.3

The **Toggle Keys** accessibility feature causes a high pitched tone to sound when the Caps Lock, Num Lock, or Scroll Lock keys are switched on and causes a low pitched tone to sound when they are turned off. Therefore, it is useful for users with visual or cognitive disabilities, making option D the correct answer.

14.D - Topic 109.4

As described in answer 20 of Practice Exam 1 and answer 48 of Practice Exam 2, **/etc/nsswitch.conf** is the name service switch configuration file, which can be used to specify the order in which hostnames are resolved. In particular, this can be done by modifying the **hosts** line, making option D the correct answer.

15.C - Topic 108.4

Based on the explanation of question 58 of Practice Exam 3, the command in option C is the right command to use to cancel the job with ID 12 from the destination printer named **Print_office_1**.

16.C - Topic 105.2

In bash, a loop construct (**for, while, until**) is a loop that executes a series of commands zero or more times. You can use the **break** command to exit from the loop immediately and the **continue** command to go to the next iteration of the loop without executing the remaining commands of the current iteration. This makes option C the correct answer. For completeness, the **quit** and **close** commands do not exist.

17.A - Topic 109.2

In many Linux distributions, the **/etc/hostname** file can be used to configure the name of the local system to be set at boot time (that is, it holds the computer's default hostname). Therefore, option A is the correct answer. For completeness, **/etc/hosts** holds mappings of IP addresses to hostnames on a single computer, while **/etc/default/hostcfg** and **/etc/default/hname** do not exist.

18.D - Topic 109.1

An IPv6 address is 128-bit long and consists of eight groups of four hexadecimal digits (numbers from 0 to 9 and letters from A to F). Leading zeroes in a group can be omitted, and one or more consecutive groups containing zeros can be compressed in a single empty group by specifying only two colons (this compression can only be applied once in the address to avoid creating an ambiguous representation). Based on these considerations, option D contains a valid IPv6 address and is therefore the correct answer. For completeness, option A applies compression twice creating an ambiguous representation, option B uses the letters g and h which are not valid hexadecimal digits, and option C specifies an address longer than 128 bits (it has eight groups of four hexadecimal digits and one or more compressed groups).

19.A, E - Topic 108.1

Network Time Protocol (NTP) is a protocol designed to keep computer clocks synchronized in a network environment. In the simplest structure, computers and network devices periodically synchronize their clock with a reference server that, in turn, receives the exact time from a definitive time source, such as an atomic clock. The purpose is to keep the clock of these network devices accurate by correcting the time drift of their system clock based on the reference server clock. In general, you can have a tiered hierarchy of time sources, but the concept is the same. This makes options A and E the correct answers.

20. B - Topic 109.3

The MTU (Maximum Transmission Unit) of a network interface is the maximum byte size of a block of data that can be sent as a single unit over the network. In Linux, you can use the **ip link set** command with the **mtu** attribute to change the maximum transmission unit of a specified network interface. Therefore, option B is the correct answer. For completeness, the **ip** command does not have the **dev** and **iface** objects, and the **addr** object does not have the **set** subcommand.

21. A - Topic 110.3

In OpenSSH clients, the **/etc/ssh/ssh_known_hosts** and **~/.ssh/known_hosts** files contain host public keys for all known hosts. In particular, **/etc/ssh/ssh_known_hosts** is a global file that should be prepared and maintained by the system administrator, while **~/.ssh/known_hosts** is a local file for a specific user account and is maintained automatically. Therefore, option A is the correct answer.

22. B - Topic 105.1

The command specified in the question assigns a new value to the **VAR** variable only for that command and then executes **echo $VAR** in a new bash shell. As a result, the command echoes **b** on the new bash shell, but if you run **echo $VAR** in the main shell, the output is still **a** (thus the value of **VAR** is not modified). Therefore, option B is the correct answer.

23. B, C - Topic 109.3

The **ifconfig** command is a traditional net-tool used to configure kernel-resident network interfaces. If no options and arguments are given, it displays the status of the currently active interfaces. If a single interface argument is given, it displays the status of the given interface (IP address, IPv6 address if assigned, hardware address, and additional statistics). If the **-a** option is given, it displays the status of all interfaces, even those that are down. Using **ifconfig**, you can, for example, set the IP address, netmask, MTU of an interface, but not the default gateway of a Linux machine (see the man pages for the complete list of activities you can do with this command). Finally, remember that **ifconfig** is now obsolete and has been replaced by the **ip** command (specifically **ip addr** and **ip link**). Therefore, options B and C are the correct answers.

24. A - Topic 107.1

The **groupdel** command is used to delete a group, making option A the correct answer. Remember that you cannot remove the primary group of any existing user, but you must remove the user before removing the group. Also remember to manually check all the files on the system to make sure that no files remain owned by the removed group.

25. D - Topic 109.4

In Linux, **dig**, **host** and **nslookup** are utilities that can be used to perform DNS lookups, converting names to IP addresses and vice versa. In particular, **dig** is flexible, easy to use, useful for performing even complex tasks, and clear in showing information broken down by sections (header, question section, answer section, authority section, additional section, stats section). For this reason, its output is normally longer than that of **nslookup** and **host** and can be very useful for troubleshooting DNS problems. Therefore, option D is the correct answer. Only for completeness, remember that the **nslookup** utility is deprecated.

26. A, B - Topic 109.2

Based on the explanation of question 25 of Practice Exam 2, ethernet and bluetooth are two valid connection types supported by NetworkManager that can be used with the **nmcli** command. Therefore, options A and B are the correct answers.

27. D - Topic 107.2

The **at** utility is used to schedule one or more commands to be executed at a specific time in the future. When you type **at** on the command line followed by a valid time specification, **at** places you at a special prompt, where you can type the commands to be executed at the scheduled time. Then if you type **CTRL+D**, you exit the special prompt, placing the scheduled job in the **at queue**. Therefore, no files should be edited to schedule an **at job**, making option D the correct answer. For completeness, remember that the **-f** option of the **at** command allows you to read an **at job** from a specified file rather than from standard input.

28.D - Topic 109.3

The **ping** command is used to verify that a host is reachable (basic network connectivity), and to isolate a fault within a network. Therefore, option D is the correct answer. For completeness, the **host** command is used to perform DNS lookups, the **traceroute** command is used to print the route packets trace to a network host, and the **ipck** command does not exist.

29.C - Topic 106.2

The VNC protocol, which stands for Virtual Network Computing, is a simple protocol used to access remote desktop sessions. Therefore, a VNC application (such as RealVNC) can be used to remotely access and control a system over a network connection, making option C the correct answer. Remember that a VNC application is very useful for helpdesk support and network administrators for troubleshooting remote systems.

30.B - Topic 110.1

In Linux, **nmap**, which stands for Network Mapper, is a useful tool commonly used for security audits. In fact, it can help you look for open ports on the local computer or on other computers within the network. This makes option B the correct answer.

31./etc/gshadow - Topic 107.1

In Linux, **/etc/gshadow** is a file of four colon-delimited fields that contains encrypted group passwords. Each line describes a single group and contains the following fields: the **group name**, the **encrypted password of the group**, the **group administrators**, and the **group members**.

32. A - Topic 108.1

The **timedatectl** command is used to query and change the system clock and its settings. In particular, the **set-time** subcommand sets the system clock to the specified time, also updating the RTC time accordingly. This makes option A the correct answer. For completeness, **timedatectl** does not have the **set-date** subcommand and the **datetimectl** command does not exist.

33. D - Topic 106.1

The **xauth** program is used to accomplish the task described in the question, making option D the correct answer. In general, this command is used to edit and display the authorization information used in connecting to the X server.

34. B - Topic 107.1

Based on the explanation of question 32 of Practice Exam 1, the group identification number of the primary group for the user in the system (GID - Group ID) is the fourth field of each line in **/etc/passwd**. Therefore, option B is the correct answer.

35. C - Topic 109.1

The MAC (Media Access Control) address is the unique hardware address of a device, primarily assigned by device manufacturers (many network interfaces support changing their MAC address). In particular, the MAC address of an Ethernet card is 48-bit long and is normally displayed as 12 hexadecimal digits. Therefore, option C is the correct answer.

36. C - Topic 107.3

The **tzselect** command is used to find out and view the installed time zones. It is invoked without parameters and asks the user for information on a specific location, showing the resulting time zone description to the standard output. Therefore, option C is the correct answer. Remember that the output of **tzselect** is suitable as a value for the **TZ** environment variable, and that you can use this command if you want to know what time it is in a specific country or what time zones exist.

37. B - Topic 108.3

The **sendmail -bi** command is equivalent to **newaliases** and is therefore used to initialize the mail alias database. Therefore, option B is the correct answer.

38. B - Topic 108.2

As described in answer 8 of the Assessment Test, in answer 50 of Practice Exam 1, and in answer 51 of Practice Exam 3, each line in the **/etc/rsyslog.conf** file takes the following form: **facility.priority action**. This syntax indicates to log all messages of the given **facility** with the specified level of **priority** or higher to a particular location. The combination of **facility** and **priority** is often referred to as a **selector**. You can define multiple **selectors** on a line, separating them with a semicolon, and you can define multiple **facilities** and **priorities** within a single **selector**, separating them with a comma. An asterisk (*) is used to define all **facilities** or **priorities**, while the **none** priority is used to indicate that no logging for the given **facility** should be done. Based on these considerations, option B is the correct answer.

39. C - Topic 110.1

In Linux, **fuser** can be used as an auditing tool to check processes using TCP/UDP sockets. In particular, if you want to see which processes are currently using network port 21 on your system, you can use one of these two syntaxes: **fuser -v 21/tcp** or **fuser -vn tcp 21**. The -v option displays all process information in one command (verbose mode), while the **-n** option allows you to select a specific namespace (tcp in the example). Therefore, option C is the correct answer. For completeness, the **pstrace** command does not exist.

40. C - Topic 107.2

In systemd, **timers** can be used as an alternative to **cron** to run tasks periodically. For each timer file, there must be a matching unit file, which represents the unit to be activated when the timer elapses (by default the service with the same name as the timer, except for the suffix). This makes option C the correct answer. For completeness, the **journal** is the systemd logging system, while **at** and **batch** are utilities to schedule and run tasks only once at a specific time in the future (one-shot).

41. A - Topic 105.2

As described in answer 10 of the Assessment Test and answer 6 of Practice Exam 3, the **test** command is a bash built-in that is used to evaluate conditional expressions. You can also use square brackets instead of **test** to perform the same tasks. In particular, the **-L** unary operator is used to perform a simple test on a specific filesystem object and returns true if the object exists and is a symbolic link, making option A the correct answer. For completeness, the **-s** unary operator returns true if the specified filesystem object exists and has size greater than zero, the **-S** unary operator returns true if the specified filesystem object exists and is a socket, and the **-f** unary operator returns true if the specified filesystem object exists and is a regular file. Finally, remember that, as with the **test** command, you can build a minimal but complete conditional test by using the **&&** operator for the **true branch** and the **||** operator for the **false branch**.

42. A - Topic 110.3

The **ssh-add** command is used to add private keys to the authentication agent. If any file requires a passphrase, **ssh-add** asks the user to enter it. This command can also be used to remove previously added identities. Therefore, option A is the correct answer. For completeness, the **ssh-keygen** command is used to generate, manage and convert authentication keys for SSH, while the **ssh-addkey**, **add-key** and **key-add** commands do not exist.

43. C - Topic 107.1

The **useradd** command is used to create new user accounts. In particular, the **-m** (**--create-home**) option also creates the new user's home directory, if it does not exist, while the **-M** option does not create the new user's home directory, even if

CREATE_HOME in **/etc/login.defs** is set to yes. Therefore, option C is the correct answer. For completeness, the **--add-home** and **--home-add** options are invalid.

44. restrict - Topic 108.1

The **restrict** directive in **/etc/ntp.conf** is used to restrict or control access to the NTP service running on a system, thus providing better security for that service.

45. A, B - Topic 108.2

As described in answer 48 of Practice Exam 1, a **facility** is the subsystem that generates a specific log message. For example, some possible values you can find in **/etc/rsyslog.conf** are **mail** and **user** which are used for mail system messages and user-level messages respectively. Therefore, options A and B are the correct answers.

46. C - Topic 105.2

Based on the explanation of question 10 of the Assessment Test, question 6 of Practice Exam 3, and question 41 of Practice Exam 4, you can use the **test** command or square brackets to perform a simple test on a specific filesystem object. In particular, the **-r** unary operator returns true if the specified filesystem object exists and is readable, the **-w** unary operator returns true if the specified filesystem object exists and is writable, the **-x** unary operator returns true if the specified filesystem object exists and is executable, and the **-e** unary operator returns true if the specified filesystem object exists. Therefore, option C is the correct answer.

47. B, C - Topic 108.2

The main log rotation configuration file is **/etc/logrotate.conf**, which specifies how log rotation and archiving should take place. This file contains general settings and usually refers to other files in the **/etc/logrotate.d** directory for managing specific logs. In particular, when configuring log rotation, you can specify many directives in these files such as **dateext** to archive old versions of logs by adding a daily extension instead of simply adding a number, and **rotate** to specify how many times log files should be rotated before being removed or mailed to a specific address. This makes options B and C the correct answers.

48. B - Topic 109.3

When DNS resolution does not work, if you simply type the **route** command on the bash prompt to find the kernel routing table, a timeout may occur because this command, by default, attempts to resolve names of routers and destinations. In such cases, the **-n** option can be very useful; in fact, it only shows the IP addresses instead of trying to find the hostnames associated with them. Therefore, option B is the correct answer. For completeness, the **route** command does not have the **-i**, **-d**, and **-a** options.

49. C - Topic 107.1

Changing the default shell of a user account to **/bin/false** prevents the user obtaining an interactive login session. Normally, the default shell for system user accounts is set to **/bin/ false** and, therefore, no one could use these accounts for direct shell access (they are not login accounts, but accounts created only to run specific tasks in the system). However, remember that other accesses are possible such as POP or IMAP. As a result, option C is the correct answer. For completeness, the **/etc/nologin** file prevents all ordinary users from logging into the system, the **nologinuser** command is invalid, and the **nologin** group does not exist by default.

50. C - Topic 108.2

In Linux, **/etc/systemd/journald.conf** is the main configuration file for the systemd-journald service. For example, in this file you can control where journal data should be stored or if it should be compressed before it is written to the file system. Therefore, option C is the correct answer.

51. D - Topic 109.2

In Linux, **nmcli** is a front-end for NetworkManager, which operates on a series of objects. In particular, the **connection** object is used to start, stop, and manage network connections and the **down** and **up** subcommands of this object are used to deactivate and activate a connection respectively (the connection is identified by its name, UUID or D-Bus path, and in case of ambiguity the keywords **id**, **uuid** or **path** can be used). Therefore, option D is the correct answer. For completeness, the **connection** object does not have the **switch** subcommand, and the **nmcli** command does not have the **disable-conn** and **enable-conn** objects.

52. A - Topic 105.1

This question is similar to question 18 of Practice Exam 3. The difference is that the **root** user defines an alias with single quotation marks, causing the shell to evaluate any variable reference at the time the alias is executed. Therefore, option A is the correct answer.

53. B - Topic 110.3

In Linux, **gpg-agent** is a program that runs in background and stores GPG private keys and their passphrase. The main advantage of using a key agent is that you don't need to type the passphrase every time you use the private key, but only once at the beginning. This makes option B the correct answer. For completeness, remember that by default a cache entry is valid for 600 seconds, unless otherwise specified.

54. B - Topic 110.2

In Linux, **/etc/hosts.allow** and **/etc/hosts.deny** are access control files used by TCP Wrappers to determine whether or not a machine is allowed to connect to a specific service. The format for an entry is as follows for both files: **DaemonList : ClientList [: command]**, where **DaemonList** is a comma-separated list of daemons, or keyword **ALL** for all daemons, **ClientList** is a comma-separated list of clients, or keyword **ALL** for all clients, and **command** is an optional command that is executed when clients try to access a server daemon. Therefore, option B is the correct answer. Refer to the man pages to see the order in which the access rules are applied.

55. A - Topic 105.1

The **set** built-in command is used to change the value of a shell option and set the positional parameters. If no options or arguments are supplied, **set** displays the names and values of all shell variables and functions. This makes option A the correct answer. For completeness, the **show_function, set_function,** and **show** commands do not exist.

56. B - Topic 109.1

CIDR notation /25 indicates that the first 25 bits of the network mask are set to 1. Therefore, it corresponds to a network mask of 255.255.255.128 (11111111.11111111.11111111.10000000), making option B the correct answer.

57. B - Topic 107.3

The **timedatectl** command is used to query and change the system clock and its settings. It accepts a series of commands such as **list-timezones** which lists the available time zones, and **set-timezone** which sets the system time zone to the specified value. This makes option B the correct answer. For completeness, the **timectl, datectl,** and **timezonectl** commands do not exist.

58. D - Topic 110.2

Based on the explanation of question 56 of Practice Exam 2 and question 46 of Practice Exam 3, encrypted passwords for users and groups are stored in **/etc/shadow** and **/etc/gshadow**, making option D the correct answer.

59. D - Topic 110.3

In Linux, it can sometimes be very useful to encrypt X connections with SSH (thus tunnel X through SSH). In particular, to enable X11 forwarding in SSH, you must invoke **ssh** with the **-X** option (or set the **ForwardX11** option to yes in the ssh client configuration file). Pay attention to the uppercase letter because the **-x** option disables X11 forwarding. If X forwarding is in effect, the **DISPLAY** variable is automatically set in the shell of the remote host. Therefore, option D is the correct answer. For completeness, remember to check that the **X11Forwarding** option is set to yes in the SSH server configuration file. Also note that you can invoke **ssh** with the **-Y** option to enable trusted X11 forwarding or you can set the **ForwardX11Trusted** option to yes in the ssh client configuration file.

60.A, B - Topic 109.2

Based on the explanation of question 39 of Practice Exam 1, **networking** and **connection** are two valid objects for the **nmcli** command. Therefore, options A and B are the correct answers.